With Love Overflowing

About The Author

Rev. Dr. Derry James-Tannariello is a retired Board Certified Chaplain, and carries a BA in Religion; BS in Personal Ministries and Psychology; MA in Christian Psychology; Master of Divinity; and Doctor of Ministry specializing in Christian Counseling. She has also been awarded VIP Woman of the Year by the National Association of Professional Women.

Derry founded Chaplain Services at Sierra Nevada Memorial Hospital in California. Hospitals, churches, educational institutions and other community organizations solicit her expertise in training others to minister to the sick and terminally ill, and for help dealing with loss and grief.

Derry is a retired healthcare chaplain, author, and sought-after speaker known for her compassionate heart, humor and life-changing inspirational stories of faith and wisdom. She is an internationally recognized seminar and workshop presenter and an interdenominational guest speaker and lecturer on topics of "How to Have an Effective Prayer Life," "Personal Transformation," "Relational God," "Spirituality and Health" and many more spiritually uplifting topics.

Derry also speaks and presents seminars on "Spiritual Support in Palliative Care," "Bereavement and Grief," "End of Life," "Ministering to Our Dying Loved Ones," "Effective Hospital Visitation" and other topics in hospital ministry.

Derry resides part-time in New Hampshire and Florida with her husband, where she assumes pastoral responsibilities, offers spiritual guidance, chaplain support, and enjoys teaching classes based upon her training and experience.

Derry has authored a number of other books, shown and described at the end of this book. To learn more about her, her other books, or to have her as a speaker for your event, workshop or organization, visit her website:

FreedomInSurrender.net

or contact her at: Derry@FreedomInSurrender.net

With *Love* Overflowing

Stories of the Incomprehensible, Irresistible Jesus

Indeed you, Lord, are kind and forgiving,
overflowing with gracious love
to everyone who calls on you.

—

Psalm 86:5 ISV

Freedom in Surrender Publishing
Amherst, New Hampshire

Derry James-Tannariello, DMin BCC

Published by Freedom in Surrender Publishing.

For book signings, bulk purchases and inquiries, contact the author at her website: FreedomInSurrender.net.

To order *With Love Overflowing* or any other titles by this author, visit: FreedomInSurrender.net.

Publisher's Cataloging-in-Publication Data
James-Tannariello, Derry

    with love overflowing : stories of the incomprehensible, irresistible jesus / by Derry James-Tannariello, DMin BCC.—1st ed.

        p. cm.

    ISBN-13: 978-1-7354208-0-6

    ISBN-10: 1-7354208-0-8

    1. Prayer. 2. Pastoral Theology. 3. Worship. 4. God-Christianity.
    5. Jesus Christ. 6. Holy Spirit. I. James-Tannariello, Derry. II. Title.

Library of Congress Control Number: 2021932260

Printed in the United States of America

Dedication

Every book I write will first of all be dedicated to the love of my life—God the Father, the Son Jesus, and the Holy Spirit, whose love has overflowed to me and given me reason to live and purpose of presence. I pray that this book will give you at least a glimpse of their extravagant love for you too.

Next, they are dedicated to my sons and their families, each of whom I love deeply and cherish always in my heart.

This book I also dedicate to my mother Dixie, who rests in Jesus. She continually reminded me that God had great things in mind for me. Her words of confidence and affirmation motivated me to forge ahead. And to my father-in-law Papa Mario who gave me the courage to keep on keeping on.

I also dedicate this book to my spiritual children inherited through the Compassion program who are now part of my life forever. May their love for Jesus make a difference in their country—their villages and cities.

And to all the passionate readers who have been hungering and thirsting to know God intimately and who long for the assurance that God knows who they are, loves them, has a plan specifically for them, and will guide them through the uncertainties of life.

God So Loved The World

—Helen Steiner Rice[†]

©Greg Olsen[‡]

Our Father Up In Heaven,
  long, long years ago,

Looked down in His great mercy
  upon the earth below

And saw that folks were lonely
  and lost in deep despair,

And so He said, "I'll send My Son
  to walk among them there ...

So they can hear Him speaking
  and feel His nearness, too,

And see the many miracles
  that Faith alone can do ...

For if man really sees Him
  and can touch His healing hand

I know it will be easier
  to Believe and Understand" ...

And so The Holy Christ Child
  came down to live on earth

And that is why we celebrate
  His Holy, wondrous birth,

And that is why at Christmas
  the world becomes aware

That heaven may seem far away
  but God Is Everywhere.

[†]©1970 Helen Steiner Rice Foundation Fund, LLC, a wholly owned subsidiary of Cincinatti Museum Center

[‡]©Greg Olsen. By arrangement with Greg Olsen Art, Inc. For information on artwork by Greg Olsen please visit www.GregOlsen.com

Contents

Preface

It has been about 45 years since God first spoke to me about writing the companion book to this book, *With Gladness Every Day*. For the full story and background, I hope you will get a copy of *With Gladness Every Day* and read the Preface.

With Kisses From Heaven came about next because of the abundance of stories I had accumulated highlighting God's magnificent love. There were more stories than could fit in *With Kisses* so now we have *With Love Overflowing*.

When I have been at a point of giving up writing, I remember the cards of encouragement given to me when I attended a Book Expo many years ago. One said, "God is with you! Expect a miracle." The picture on it was of a baby duck standing up sticking the tip of its little webbed toes in the water. The other was a picture of a little mouse about to grab the cheese from a mousetrap. It said, "Only go through the doors God opens." I sensed God prompting—encouraging me that He would speak through me and help me accomplish this task. I have carried these cards ever since. They have been a reminder that God gave me the title *With Gladness Every Day* because He had a book in mind and has since cleared the way for more books to follow.

Over these past 45 years God has been developing the content through His interventions in my life and in the lives of those I love, by my life experiences, spiritual growth, answered prayers and interventions of His saving grace and incomprehensible love. Now with God's promptings I have put these stories together to bring hope to a troubled world and encouragement to suffering hearts.

Over the last few years you would have found me writing stories while riding in the car as we traveled the east coast, snuggled in a corner of the guest room to escape the noise and distractions around me, sitting at the dining room table with papers spread out all over the table—piled on the floor and stacked in groups on the counters. When we went out on the boat—I had my tablet with me. Out on the lanai or patio at the campground with my computer—stories were pouring forth. Early morning hours and late night hours, whenever the inspiration came, I tried to capture the moment. Sometimes after a dream, I would awake and scribble notes on my notepad in the dark. Wherever we went I took a file box of stories and notes that needed to be organized and reworked. My husband will be thrilled when I wrap this up. Half of our house will be purged from clutter and excess baggage! As I write this, we are now dry camping. The water was shut off over a week ago and still … I write.

I have been completing this manuscript and the companion books *With Gladness Every Day* and *With Kisses From Heaven* during the 2020 pandemic. Looting and rioting are out of control. Our world is mired in fear and despair with all the terrorism. God has chosen the writing of these books for such a time as this. This is a time in history when people want to know God is real. He cares about this world and He delights to answer prayer and as we believe in Him—prove Himself faithful.

I would like to acknowledge and thank Ray Fusci, a gifted editor and designer who has blessed me with his many talents, direction, sacrificial labor and professional knowledge. Calvin Coolidge once said, "No person was ever honored for what he received. Honor has been the reward for what he gave." Today, I honor Ray Fusci knowing that God will reward him for all he has done to help put these experiences in print to encourage others in their journey and quest to grow in Jesus. He was also instrumental in the completion and success of previous books I have written. You will find these listed at the end of this book.

I also want to thank my husband Ron for his patience waiting through times when the need to complete this project has interfered with his desire to do other things. He has been supportive and attentive to my needs. Thank you, my love.

Thomas Jefferson said, "Every human mind feels pleasure in doing good to another." All I can say is these precious friends do so much good they must feel a tremendous amount of pleasure!

Thank you each one with sincere love and deepest appreciation. God bless you over and over.

Birthed from over 50 years of living life and experiencing God, it is with joy I present to you *With Love Overflowing*.

That Overflowing love is how God is with you always, and no matter what.
—Cyndi Wunder

Introduction

Frequently after I have spoken at a seminar or conference, I have been asked if I have written a book containing my stories. I am finally doing just that. *With Love Overflowing* now completed, I have the third companion book sharing stories of God's incomprehensible, unrelenting, exorbitant love. *With Gladness Every Day* is divided into "Answers to Prayer" and "Life Experiences." *With Kisses From Heaven* is divided into "God's Intervention" and "Scripture Lessons." *With Love Overflowing* includes stories of God's saving grace and all knowing wisdom and plans. All stories illustrate God's extravagant love and His limitless ways of manifesting that love to us.

The desire of my heart is to help show that Jesus is alive today!!! He is a caring and loving God Who hears and answers prayer, longs to make Himself known to His children, and builds relationship with each of us. If you are having difficulty developing a personal relationship with Him, or believing He answers prayer, I recommend reading His #1 best seller, *The Bible*. I would also refer you to my books *Praying in the "Yes" of God* and *Growing in the "Yes" of God,* which can help you implement what you study.

Throughout the books I have written you will read "God said" or "I heard" or some other similar expression. When I say that, it doesn't mean I heard an audible voice (although at times I have). I am referring to that inner voice He speaks quietly to your mind or heart; sometimes it is a 'knowing' or a 'sense of His presence.' Sometimes God speaks through friends but He lets you know in your heart it is from Him. Sometimes you will recognize His voice through what you read in Scripture or inspirational books, through music, nature, or providential workings. God has many ways of "speaking" to us and making sure we hear Him. In this book, I hope to 'whet your appetite' for more of Him by sharing how involved He is in every aspect of our lives.

With Love Overflowing

Life happens; the challenges and the joys. Do we just make it through each day or do we stop a minute to reflect? What happened today? How did I see God in this? What can I learn from today's experience? Is there anything I need to change? Anything I need to take care of? Anyone I need to address?

Every day is a new day of life and opportunities. We can make it by barely hanging on or we can learn, grow, love, share and make a difference for good. In this world of chaos, we are looking for security and love we can depend upon, an expressed unconditional love. *With Love Overflowing* shares stories that confirm there is security in Jesus and peace during life's turmoil and storms.

I hope these encounters resonate with you and open your eyes to the many ways God has proven Himself present in your life and shown His interest in all that concerns you.

My purpose for these books is a reminder to myself and, I hope, to impress upon your heart, that our God is a personal, caring God Who loves you extravagantly with overwhelming, incomprehensible love and is aware of everything that concerns you. He is there for you, even in silence.

I pray that as you read of my failings and victories, you will gain confidence that Jesus offers you victory as well. May my life sharing offer you convincing proof that God is aware of all that concerns you and will work mightily in your behalf.

No matter how you feel or what you've done; no matter how far away God seems, He is right by your side. Every day can be a day of new beginnings as you experience His forgiveness, outpouring of His unlimited love, and divine interventions when you most need them.

Jesus came to offer you life more abundantly and hope for every tomorrow. When you find in Him all this and more, He will become to you truly irresistible. You will desire to be more like Him and your love for others will overflow as did His.

Love Overflowing

In this world of chaos, we are looking for security; that place free from fear, a place where we know we are loved unconditionally and will be cared for no matter what. I found that place in the incomprehensible, irresistible, overflowing love and protection of Jesus the Savior Who mirrors the majesty of God, our Father. May your heart be awakened to learn and understand more of Him and to experience Him for yourself.

It was suggested that I not use the subtitle Stories of the Incomprehensible, Irresistible Jesus. I was told that if Jesus were irresistible everyone would be following and embracing Him. There is a truth to that, but I still disagree. When you realize all He has done and sacrificed for you, when you really know Jesus as a personal friend and experience Him in your life, He does become irresistible! His love is incomprehensible beyond anything you have experienced or can imagine.

After learning of Him, you will want to live your life in a way that will honor Him and reflect His character. He lived unselfishly bringing His love and hope to others to relieve their suffering and offered understanding and encouragement. As you contemplate Him, your life will take on new meaning—all because you recognize and have experienced His love overflowing in everything that concerns you.

As you read these stories of His outpouring and overflowing love, may you sense His personal caring. If you will honor God, there is no power that can stand against you. If you take hold of Jesus—everything will change. I pray your heart will be awakened to learn and understand more of Him and to experience Him for yourself. May you, as I, find Him truly irresistible.

With Love Overflowing

Somebody Loves You
—Helen Steiner Rice[†]

Somebody loves you more than you know,
Somebody goes with you wherever you go,
Somebody really and truly cares
And lovingly listens to all of your prayers …

Don't doubt for a minute
    that this is not true,
For God loves His children
    and takes care of them, too …
And all of His treasures
    are yours to share
If you love Him completely
    and show Him you care …
And if you "walk in His footsteps"
    and have the faith to believe,
There's nothing you ask for
    that you will not receive.

©2021 Danny Hahlbohm, www.inspiredart.store

[†]©1976 Helen Steiner Rice Foundation Fund, LLC, a wholly owned subsidiary of Cincinatti Museum Center

As a father has compassion on his children, so the
LORD has compassion on those who fear him;
—Psalm 103:13 NIV

A "Daddy" Surprise

Sometimes a young girl, because of circumstances in her life, has to grow up without a dad or without a close relationship with her dad. When that happens, it can leave a hole in her heart, a void she never expects to have filled. I'm not talking about the place only Jesus fills, or any place that runs competition with Jesus; I'm just talking about the need a child has for "Daddy."

My biological father died at the age of 37. I was only 13. It was particularly difficult for me because I was the oldest child and I was his favorite. My mother preferred my second sister. Things changed for both of us when more children came along five years later.

Daddy would take me to work with him and made me feel important by having me help in the office with filing and putting his paperwork in order. I would get to tag along with him on hunting trips where he taught me how to shoot his big rifle. When he was home, his lap was always available and so were his arms.

But Dad had his problems, too. He wasn't home much and he was an alcoholic. He was also unfaithful to my mom.

1

With Love Overflowing

Midway through their divorce he died in bed with his mistress. I was left with many scars and many broken dreams.

There was no man in my life who could guide, protect and counsel this young girl; answer her questions and give her advice; attend the father/daughter events at school. My uncle graciously walked me down the aisle at my wedding, but it should have been my dad.

Mother remarried several years later, but by then I was already out of the house and on my own. While I called her husband Dad, and loved him, he never really "fathered" me, except for once when he actually sat and listened to my heart and gave me some advice. That happened when *I* went through a very painful divorce.

When I remarried at the age of 62 after being alone for over 12 years, I received a bonus, an unexpected gift of a father figure. It was almost more than I could conceive. God gave me a man who accepted me and loved me as his daughter.

Little girls can run to their daddy and cry. I found out that big girls can, too. When my heart ached with grief because of my separation from family and close friends thousands of miles away, my longing for the ministry and security I had left behind, my confusion about my new life, my exhaustion from trying to settle in, I could go to Papa. I could say, Daddy, I don't want to talk about my pain, I just need a hug. He would hold me tight and stroke my head and say, it's going to be alright, Honey. Be patient.

A "Daddy" Surprise

When I needed help with a project, whether it was struggling through the directions to see how to put together the bookshelves in the basement or setting up my office at the school, Papa was there by my side. We worked, we laughed, we decided how we were going to do the job, and eventually...got it done. If something were too heavy for us, somehow together we got the job accomplished by much innovation.

Papa became my "Daddy" as well as my dear friend. He gave advice, encouraged me, bragged about me, intervened for me, and most importantly to me; he loved me and was proud of me.

We used to sit at the table, share stories and memories, and have deep spiritual discussions. He would share questions he had been hiding in his heart and listen intently to my responses. Heart sharing was something I had missed for a very long time.

My new husband, his son, had a boat and loved to go to the lake. Papa loved to go places with us, but wasn't real keen about the water. He was afraid to go in; until; after much coaxing; I finally persuaded him to come in and play. Little by little he pushed himself until he let us hold him up so he could lie on his back.

Papa was 92. I didn't realize at the time that he was building up his courage so he could be baptized. What an exciting experience that was! What joy! Can you imagine the influence a man of 92 had on others by humbling himself and making a decision to be baptized at that age?

I was thinking about all of this today; about how life robs us and blesses us. I was thinking about how when we least expect it, God just surprises us with something we have longed for and missed.

While God, our Father, is always with us, He loves to extend His love to us through others. In Psalm 68:5 He tells us He will be *A father of the fatherless, a defender of widows,* Is *God in*

With Love Overflowing

His holy habitation. He did this for me when He gave me Papa; His arms through human arms to love this girl and heal her heart. He is also there for you; waiting for just the right moment.

Love Overflowed:

I see the importance of loving. Love begets love. I experienced my Father in heaven, Who has promised to be a Father to the fatherless, compassionately show me love through an earthly father figure, my daddy surprise! Thank You, Father God.

He defends the cause of the fatherless and the widow, and loves the foreigner residing among you, giving them food and clothing.
—Deuteronomy 10:18 NIV.

Do you need a Father who loves you unconditionally and will never fail you? Look to God.

4

For He shall give His angels charge over you, To keep you in all your ways. In their hands they shall bear you up, Lest you dash your foot against a stone.
—Psalm 91:11-12

Angel Switched Lanes

The traffic was heavy. We had been driving bumper to bumper for over an hour. I was on my way home from a full day of Chaplain's training and work at the hospital. I was tired and hungry.

When the traffic cleared and we started moving—we moved! I turned the music on in the car and settled in for the rest of the drive, but remained alert. Things wouldn't be so stressful now.

The traffic had been moving for about 15 minutes when about three car lengths in front of me was a stopped car right in the fast lane...the lane I was traveling in. I quickly checked my rear view mirror. There was a truck and trailer barreling down on me. I turned to check the right lane next to me. There was no way to pull into that lane and around this car. Traffic was moving fast and close. All I could do was cry out to Jesus and brace myself for impact. I was thinking fast. I pumped my breaks twice hoping the truck would see my warning and slow down and I was trying to slow to keep from hitting the stopped car.

With Love Overflowing

Telling the story is taking longer than all of this actually happened. I must have shut my eyes in expectation of collision because the next thing I remember is looking down the road in the right lane with the truck and trailer still behind me. Did you catch that? The right lane! There's power in the name of Jesus!

I don't know what God did or how He did it, but there I was—one lane over—safe and still moving. As I kept driving, I prayed for the protection of the people in the stopped car, trusting God to save them as well; and thanked God for saving my life.

Love Overflowed:

My life was prolonged. I have no idea how God did it. I'm assuming that even though I didn't feel like I was flying; the angels must have picked me up and moved me over when the angel switched lanes. Whatever happened, God wasn't finished with me yet and I am here to tell the story ... still in awe ... still wondering how it all came about. What incomprehensible love!

But the Lord is faithful, and He will strengthen and protect you from the evil one.—2 Thessalonians 3:3 NASB.

Have you experienced the power of calling upon the name of Jesus? When you cry out to Him, He is there.

When it rises up, the mighty are terrified; they retreat before its thrashing.—Job 41:25 NIV

Angry Alligator

We were on vacation in Florida. It had been suggested that we visit a state park and wildlife preserve that offered a tour across the lake on an airboat. That sounded interesting ... and proved to be so.

While we waited for the tour to begin, we enjoyed a bite of lunch at the restaurant upstairs. We chose a seat by the window. From our vantage point we had a view of the lake where we could watch the tour boats arriving and leaving. We also enjoyed watching a variety of birds as we were visiting with other guests who were waiting for the tour.

With Love Overflowing

Finally our time came and we boarded the boat. My husband and I chose a place near the front. After the tour guide gave us an introduction and instructions to keep all body parts inside the boat, we were ready to shove off.

Excitement welcomed us at the very start of this voyage! As soon as the engines started up, an angry, hostile alligator raised its threatening head—snarling, showing its teeth and slapping its tail!

It jumped out of the water and we could see its head over the side of the boat. My heart was pounding. It was such a surprise and scare we couldn't help but let out a scream.

I was thinking, we are in an airboat. Can that alligator take a bite out of the bottom and sink the "ship?"

The captain of the boat didn't seem upset. He had encountered this before. He steered a straight course and soon we departed from the dock.

I was stupefied by his reaction—forward ho! Once we got underway he explained. This mother alligator had a nest of several babies. She was just protecting them!

As we continued on the tour, we were told that there were thousands of alligators that lived just below the boat. They don't like wind in their noses, so on a windy day they

8

hide out under the water. The water was so shallow that occasionally the bottom of the boat would brush over one and wake it up. It would come out growling and slapping its tail.

We learned that you can tell how long an alligator is by estimating the length between the center of his eyes to his nostrils. Translate the inches into feet for an estimate of his entire length. So for example: If it were eight inches from the center of its eyes to its nostrils—it would be eight feet long!

Our short venture around the lake was indeed an experience. As I reflected on the viciousness of the alligators, particularly the mother protecting her young, I redirected my thoughts to my Heavenly Father. His love is protective and saving! Scripture promises came to mind.

Though I walk in the midst of trouble, You will revive me; You will reach out with Your hand against the wrath of my enemies, And Your right hand will save me.—Psalm 138:7 NASB.

Our world is in a state of confusion and unrest. We face the unexpected every day. Terrorism and destruction abound. We have suffered a chemical and biological attack on our country, an attempt to overthrow our government and change our nation. Life on this earth as we have known it is rapidly changing. But we serve a God Who loves us and is victorious against evil. He will fight our enemies and He has a plan for our eternal future.

The LORD goes out like a mighty man, like a man of war he stirs up his zeal; he cries out, he shouts aloud, he shows himself mighty against his foes.—Isaiah 42:13 ESV.

But the LORD is with me as a dread warrior; therefore my persecutors will stumble; they will not overcome me. They will be greatly shamed, for they will not succeed. ...—Jeremiah 20:11 ESV.

With Love Overflowing

Where does our help come from? It comes from God. Do you need His protection; the assurance of His presence? Ask Him. He is anxious to prove Himself to you.

My help comes from the LORD, Who made heaven and earth. The LORD will protect you from all evil; He will keep your soul. The LORD will guard your going out and your coming in From this time and forever.—Psalm 121:2, 7-8 NASB.

Love Overflowed:

Thank You Father for the example of the angry alligator. It reminded me how much You love us and how we have nothing to fear because in that unflinching, courageous love, You will rise up to protect us.

... perfect love casts out fear, ...—1 John 4:18.

If you are fearful, turn to Jesus. Let your heart be at peace. He will provide. He has an answer. He is the answer.

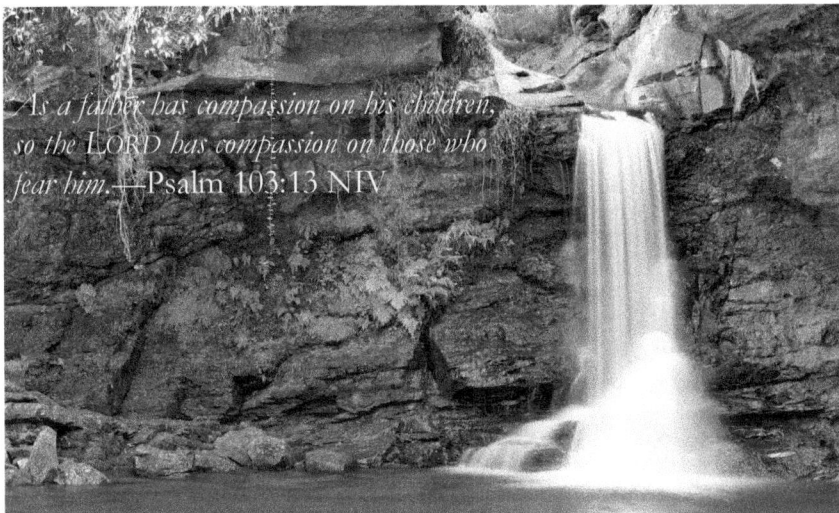

As a father has compassion on his children, so the LORD has compassion on those who fear him.—Psalm 103:13 NIV

Asleep At The Wheel

Honor your father and your mother, that your days may be long upon the land which the LORD your God is giving you.—Exodus 20:12.

I homeschooled my sons for 16 years. When they were in their senior year of high school we encouraged them to attend the nearby Christian boarding school. We remembered how much fun we had in our senior year and hoped they wouldn't miss out on some special memories.

One of our sons, Geoffrey, asked to change schools in his junior year. After my husband and I discussed his request, we felt there was no reason to deny him. He was very mature for his age. He was spiritually grounded; a man of integrity, good to his word. Scholastically his GPA was 4.0. He had good common sense as well as being intellectually astute. He related well socially and was fun to be around, bringing light-hearted wit to conversations.

It was a good decision in his case. He did well and made friends quickly. He achieved Valedictorian of his senior class.

With Love Overflowing

His absence at home had left an empty spot though. He had always been helpful, loving and fun—oh so much fun. His quick wit often brought laughter and lightened the atmosphere. I missed him terribly. But in truth, I missed each son when they left home.

I am a prayer intercessor for each of them. When they were away at school or out on their own, they often were prayed for many times a day. Anytime they were confronted with a difficult or dangerous situation, God would put it on my heart to pray for them, sometimes for hours at a time.

One day, I suddenly felt an urgency to pray for Geoffrey. I immediately stopped what I was doing and began praying, and praying, with intensity and then pleading. When I was released from the need to pray, I had peace, and curiosity. I checked the clock. I wondered what had happened to him during that time and was anxious to find out. I didn't have to wait very long. I received a phone call from him a few hours later.

When he called we chatted casually at first, then he asked if I had prayed for him. I told him what happened and what time I had been praying. He told me he knew I had. As he was traveling back to the school he had fallen asleep at the wheel. He remembered big trucks by his side, but woke up off the road safely in a ditch, which he was able to drive right out of.

Our son had generally been respectful and honoring of us, his parents, and God promises in Exodus 20:12 that if you *Honor your father and your mother, that your days may be long upon the land which the LORD your God is giving you.*

God had prompted me to pray and He had protected my son's life. No small wonder. He makes a valuable contribution to the lives of those he chooses to bless. In high school he had been part of a missionary team. As a health evangelist, he presented at seminars with skill and charisma. God has a strong calling on his life. No wonder he has encountered such disappointment and heartache. He is a threat to the enemy.

12

This was not the first time God had saved his life. When he was small he almost drowned. At the last moment he was discovered and quickly pulled out of the pool. CPR was administrated diligently until, thank God, he spewed out water and was revived.

The enemy has tried a number of times to pluck him away from God. May God be victorious in his life and may he continue to succeed as a holy, bold man of God.

Love Overflowed:

God puts His Word above His throne and His promises are true. To this day I thank God for sparing my son's life again. His giftings and innate talents were given to be a blessing to the Kingdom of God. I pray they will glorify You Jesus.

For I know the thoughts that I think toward you, says the LORD, thoughts of peace and not of evil, to give you a future and a hope.
—Jeremiah 29:11.

Are you walking in God's will and destiny for your life? God has a plan and purpose for each person. If you have not yet discovered your purpose, spend some time alone with God and ask Him to reveal it to you. When He does, don't run from it. Don't fall asleep at the wheel. When God calls, He enables and your joy will be full!

and the grace of our Lord overflowed, along with the faith and love that are in Christ Jesus. This saying is trustworthy and deserving of full acceptance: ...—1 Timothy 1:14-15 CSB.

... To comfort all who mourn, To console those who mourn in Zion, To give them beauty for ashes, The oil of joy for mourning, The garment of praise for the spirit of heaviness; That they may be called trees of righteousness, The planting of the LORD, that He may be glorified.
—Isaiah 61:2-3

Blessings From Heartache

My sisters and I did not have the privilege of growing up together. Years, time, life and different interests seemed to keep us apart. When we were younger and in close proximity, it seemed that the enemy often got the upper hand, bringing misunderstandings and division in our relationships. It wasn't until we lost our mother that things really changed significantly. The heartache and confusion that accompanied Mom's death set us on a path of discovery—of each other and self.

Our love for each other has grown and formed a very close bond. No matter what is ahead in this life—we have each other's back.

I was thinking of people in general. It is a sorry thing that too often we take each other for granted; that we don't intentionally devote time to knowing our relatives and neighbors—to discover who they are, what is important to them, what they enjoy, what their needs or dreams are. It is sad to me that often we are too self absorbed, or too insecure, to put ourselves out there—put others before ourselves.

But we have excuses—life—busy-ness, etc. We lose so many rich and valuable moments all because we are so intent

15

on fulfilling the demands of the day. How many opportunities are lost in having our own life enriched because we are too busy to invest in enriching someone else? If we would only take the time to build relationships and learn from one another.

God talks about the church being a "body" in several books of the Bible. One is found in Romans 12:4-5 ASV which says, *For even as we have many members in one body, and all the members have not the same office: so we, who are many, are one body in Christ, and severally members one of another.*

I think we could look at a family similarly. For whatever reasons, God chose us to be in the family we are in—whether it is our biological family or a God given one. If we learn to be concerned for each other's salvation, and move within the relationship with a forgiving spirit, we will be less offended. We may even find ways of sharing Jesus and bring hope and reconciliation in the family—or church unit. It is sad to me that much too often we wait until a crisis to turn to God—or to each other.

I love and cherish my sisters. I hope and pray that we will spend eternity together. No offense is worth losing heaven or cutting ourselves off from another hurting soul. If we respond to each other in hurtful ways, it is usually because we are broken and hurting ourselves. Inflicting hurt on each other is often, but not always, unintentional. None of us have wings or a halo yet. Let's give each other grace and show each other mercy.

Love Overflowed:

Father, thank You for turning mourning into something that has healed and strengthened relations among my sisters and me, for exchanging the spirit of heaviness for the garment of praise and for opening us to deeper love and understanding of one another through Your love for us. We love You, too.

16

Whom in your family do you need to reach out to, or make amends to? Jesus can give you the opportunity and the words to speak. Ask Him to help. Forgiveness is not an option. Jesus tells us if we do not forgive, He will not forgive us. If you are just learning about Jesus, this might be a difficult decision for you to make if you have been badly hurt. But I promise you, it is the first step to freedom and new life.

Our Lord is coming soon. Be ready by making "intentional" decisions. Every day keep your eyes focused on your goal—heaven—eternity with Jesus. Direct everything you do towards that goal. Make intentional choices to respond like Jesus would, do what He would do, and act like He would act. Don't waste any time and don't let anyone get in your way. May the hope of His glory shine down on you. Receive blessings from the heartaches you have experienced.

What More Can You Ask

—Helen Steiner Rice[†]

God's love endureth forever—
What a wonderful thing to know
When the tides of life run against you
And your spirit is downcast and low …

God's kindness is ever around you,
Always ready to freely impart
Strength to your faltering spirit,
Cheer to your lonely heart …

©Greg Olsen[‡]

God's presence is ever
    beside you,
As near as the reach of
    your hand.
You have but to tell Him
    your troubles,
There is nothing He
    won't understand …

And knowing God's love
    is unfailing,
And His mercy unending
    and great,
You have but to trust in His promise—
"God comes not too soon nor too late" …

So wait with a heart that is patient
For the goodness of God to prevail—
For never do prayers go unanswered,
And His mercy and love never fail.

[†]©1967 Helen Steiner Rice Foundation Fund, LLC, a wholly owned subsidiary of Cincinatti Museum Center

[‡]©Greg Olsen By arrangement with Greg Olsen Art, Inc. For information on artwork by Greg Olsen please visit www.GregOlsen.com

Behold, this day I am going the way of all the earth. And you know in all your hearts and in all your souls that not one thing has failed of all the good things which the LORD your God spoke concerning you. All have come to pass for you; not one word of them has failed.—Joshua 23:14

Cash Your Check

Living in the knowledge that Jesus knows who I am by name and desires to be in relationship with me by proving Himself real, has changed my life. The joy of communing with Him in prayer by pouring out my heart, needs and desires, and interceding for others has proven the miraculous love of the Lord. 2 Peter 1:3-4 says, *as His divine power has given to us all things that* pertain *to life and godliness, through the knowledge of Him who called us by glory and virtue, by which have been given to us exceedingly great and precious promises, that through these you may be partakers of the divine nature, having escaped the corruption* that is *in the world through lust.*

There are certain conditions the Lord expects us to fulfill with His help, if we desire the blessing, or gift, that accompanies His promises. We have no power of ourselves to fulfill the conditions. We are to present each condition to Him, as a promise for fulfillment, so that the Bible promises/scriptures we are personalizing may be received. (For a teaching on claiming Bible promises and fulfilling the conditions, see my books *Praying in the "Yes" of God* and *Growing in the "Yes" of God*.)

With Love Overflowing

Here is an example to show what I mean. Let's say that a close friend of yours knows that yesterday you received $500.00. Today this friend has an emergency. Your friend comes to see you, and says, "I hate to ask you this. I know that yesterday you received some money; and I am really desperate. Could you please loan me $100.00?"

You say, "Oh, I just put that money in the bank. I'll write you a check." So you write a check for $100.00.

Your friend will go to the bank to cash your check. When he takes the check to the teller, he won't say, "If it is your will, please give me $100.00."

The teller will say, "If you want this money, you must endorse the check." That is the condition you need to fulfill in order to get this money.

Our Father in Heaven loves us so much, He wants us to know He has blessings waiting to bestow on us. He has promises like blank checks that have already been signed in the name of Jesus, with no expiration date. Behind God's checks stand the resources of heaven and His untarnished reputation. You search His Holy Word for the promise/scripture applicable to your need. In order to receive that gift, you need to fulfill the conditions. This "is not a 'magical' way of getting what we want. Ogilvie's book 'God's Best for My Life, January 15' states "Prayer is to get us into the position of willingness to receive what God wants." This is obedience to God's instruction, *and being fully convinced that what He had promised He was also able to perform.* (Romans 4:21)

Scripture is filled with God's promises for both blessings and threats. Both are conditional for fulfillment. God waits for us to fulfill our part of complying with those conditions. He is eager to bless us!

He is so willing to give to us abundantly. I wonder if He is hurt or insulted when we pray, but fail to obey. If we are not willing to fulfill the conditions God outlines for His promise, the promise is not for us. It is for the one who obeys God's conditions.

As we consider praying for a particular request, we might be less hesitant if we would remember that we serve a God of love Who has filled the Bible with promises to encourage us and give us hope. We serve a Father Who, because of His extravagant love, desires to bestow good gifts upon His children. He desires that our joy be full.

Answers to prayer are not dependent upon our feelings. They are based upon the trustworthiness of our Savior and our faith in Him. His word is sure. Scripture says in Psalm 138:2, *I will worship toward Your holy temple, And praise Your name For Your lovingkindness and Your truth; For You have magnified Your word above all Your name.* God is eager to give us insight and instruction in how to pray effectively. He wants you to share your heart with Him and to listen to what He wants to share with you.

Be anxious for nothing, but in everything by prayer and supplication, with thanksgiving, let your requests be made known to God; (Philippians 4:6). This scripture is a promise and a command.

Love Overflowed:

Our Heavenly Father is eager to pour blessings into our lives. He wants to build our faith as He has us work in partnership with Him to give us those blessings. He is a God who doesn't lie and wants us to realize every good and perfect gift comes from His hands. He has an inexhaustible supply in heaven.

For all the promises of God in Him are *Yes, and in Him Amen, to the glory of God through us.*—2 Corinthians 1:20.

Are you ready to "cash in" on God's promises? Working in partnership with Him is a wonderful way to build a relationship. Pray through scripture. Go cash your check!

When we prevail in unceasing prayer we are abiding in continual union with God wherein love flows and abounds.

—Derry Tannariello

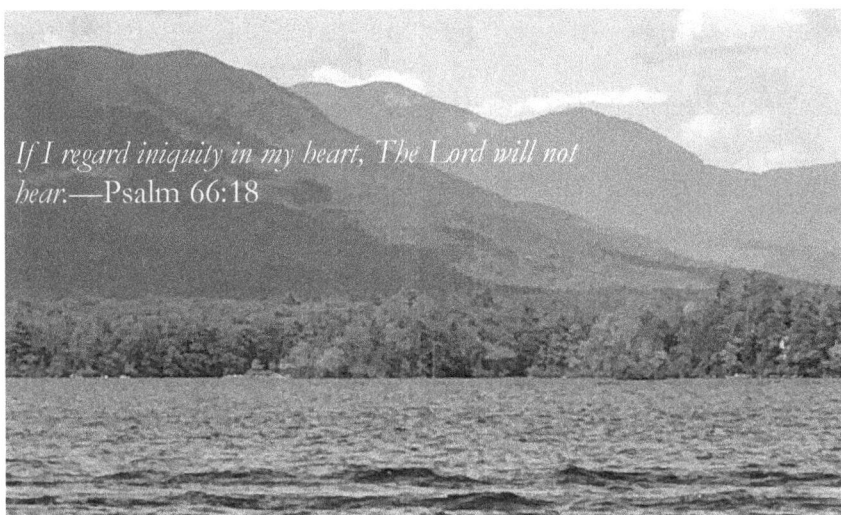

Chocoholic And Soap Operas

I was a new Christian in my mid twenties, when I realized I was a chocoholic. That means I loved chocolate. In fact, I loved chocolate so much; I drove 30 minutes to buy a five-pound box of See's candy. By the time I got home, it was almost gone. The rest I would hide around the house for my next "fix." I had it pretty bad. You may laugh, but this was a serious addiction.

Is eating a piece of chocolate a sin? That's not what I'm saying. Anything in excess is. Addiction is! I was addicted. This was a secret sin, and I had to ask Jesus for help.

God loves us and doesn't want a breach in His relationship with us so He gives the specific instruction that *If I regard iniquity in my heart, the Lord will not hear me.* Does that actually mean what it says, that if we harbor secret sin in our life, God will not hear us? This text points out secret sin is a hindrance to having our prayers answered. I don't want to hold on to anything that would come between God and me. God's word is full of promises and commands. Every command is also a promise, because when God asks us to do something He will enable us to do it. So if He gives us a command, He

23

promises to help us obey. As I presented this command to God, I asked that He would reveal anything hidden in my heart that I have been unable to see. Because He loves me, He will.

I'm ashamed to have to admit God revealed another very embarrassing addiction I was living with back then—watching soap operas. I was so hooked on them, I used to plan doctor appointments for the children and my grocery shopping all around getting back in time so I didn't miss one day of the programs. The happenings of those people had become part of my life. I had to ask God to help me let go of that. I had to be open to change in my life.

Our Father expects us to come to Him, confess our sins, and make things right. One sin, allowed to be cherished in our life, can rob us of God's anointing spirit and blessing. 1 John 1:8 cautions, *If we say that we have no sin, we deceive ourselves, and the truth is not in us.* Sin not only removes us from prayer's power but steals our joy. When we confess our sins we are promised in 1 John 1:9, *He is faithful and just to forgive us our sins and to cleanse us from all unrighteousness.*

Are we to believe we must be without sin in order for God to hear us? No. God is eager for us to confess our faults and ask for forgiveness. With fervent love, He also longs for us to make a complete surrender of anything in our life that would come between Him and us. That means we are to relinquish any hidden sins. We are to have nothing between us and our Savior—not chocolate, soap operas, addictions, wrong attitudes, or anything else. It should be Jesus first, remembering that He was crucified for others as well as for us.

Ezekiel 36:26-27 KJV promises us *A new heart also will I give you, and a new spirit will I put within you: and I will take away the stony heart out of your flesh, and I will give you a heart of flesh. And I will put my spirit within you, and cause you to walk in my statutes, and ye shall keep my judgments, and do them.*

Love Overflowed:

Renunciation is the willingness to give up our secret sins, to let go of them. I now more often ask God to search my heart and point out anything in me that makes Him sad. I want to know what His perspective is so I can keep my heart pure and without secret sin. He lovingly wants to perfect all that concerns me—chocoholic and soap opera addictions, or anything else that interferes with my relationship with Him—and draw me closer to Himself; which is exactly where I want to be!

If we cherish sin in our heart we are assured that God will not answer. Proverbs 28:9 KJV warns us, *He that turneth away his ear from hearing the law, even his prayer shall be an abomination.* That is a pretty strong word—abomination.

How does it make you feel to think that if you are holding on to some known sin, God has turned away from you and is insulted by your communication to Him? It's time to let go! Talk to Jesus about it and get things cleared up.

He who has the Holy Spirit in his heart and the
Scripture in his hands has all he needs.
—Alexander Maclaren

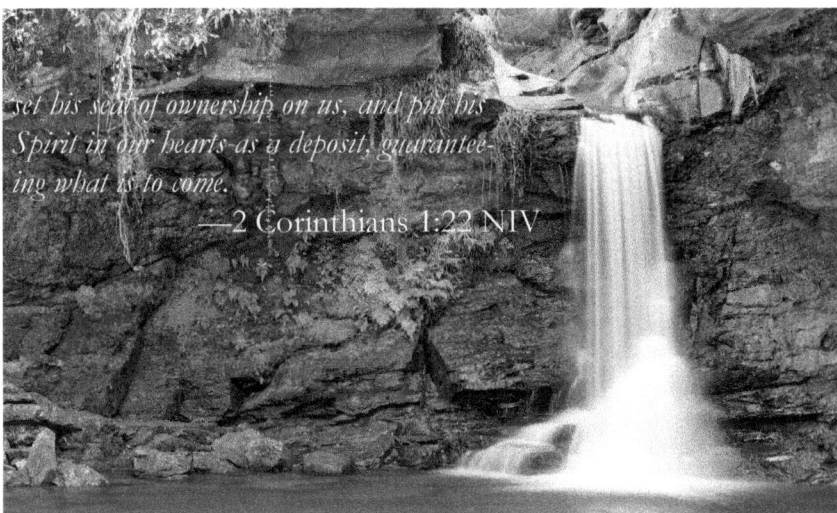

set his seal of ownership on us, and put his Spirit in our hearts as a deposit, guaranteeing what is to come.

—2 Corinthians 1:22 NIV

Deposit Of The Spirit

Many years ago, after much prayer and continual searching, we found our "dreamland." We had been looking for that "perfect spot" to build our new home. House plans were soon in hand.

I remember going out to approve an undeveloped parcel and looking across the street, pointing up the hill, I said to the realtor, "Too bad that piece wasn't for sale. I love it from here."

After a few minutes of investigating, the realtor announced, "It is!" We headed across the street to really check it out. We loved it! My husband and I immediately put a deposit on the property to secure it for ourselves. After all the time we had invested in this search we didn't want anyone else to snatch it out from under us.

What joy and relief we felt when our deposit was accepted securing the property. The risk of losing it had diminished. It was already precious to us. The future looked hopeful.

If *you* were looking for a piece of property you would have certain stipulations or criteria according to your family needs and lifestyle. Depending upon the size of your family you might have a number of variables. You may be looking for a place close to town, or schools or close to a church. Maybe you are considering living way out in the country not close to anything. Perhaps you had an idea of how much acreage you wanted, whether it had a view and good water. Any number of things would be under consideration.

Finally you find that dream parcel after looking for months. It meets your criteria. You are so excited. The first thing you would do is put a deposit, earnest money, a down payment, on that piece of property to insure that it would be yours until you can work out the rest of the details and take possession of it.

That's what Jesus has done for us. He has given the Holy Spirit as a deposit in our hearts, a down payment to insure we are His, to remind us He is coming back to redeem us; to take possession of us for eternity. Ephesians 1:13-14 tells us, *In Him you also* trusted, *after you heard the word of truth, the gospel of your salvation; in whom also, having believed, you were sealed with the Holy Spirit of promise, who is the guarantee of our inheritance until the redemption of the purchased possession, to the praise of His glory.* What a fantastic realization!

Do you realize that every time you get discouraged and depressed and wonder if Jesus cares, the very fact that your thoughts turn to God, even momentarily, that you are wondering, is assurance for you of Jesus "deposit" of the Holy Spirit working on your heart. That is your assurance He's still there. That's the deposit. Jesus reminder He is coming again. He wants to take you home. Jesus experiences joy when we accept the "deposit."

Blessed thought—Jesus wants us for Himself. He wants to make sure that we are not snatched from Him. His "earnest money" is to keep from losing us. He loves us so much. What a wonderful Jesus. What a wonderful God. What exorbitant love! Thank You Lord for Your investment in us *until the redemption of the purchased possession unto the praise of Your glory.* We love You. Our eyes are focused on You and our vision of an eternal home is rooted in heaven.

Who hath also sealed us, and given the earnest of the Spirit in our hearts.—2 Corinthians 1:22 KJV.

God's gift of the Holy Spirit is to enable us to share our love and testimony for Jesus. Our Father God tells us in Luke 11:13, to ask Him for the Holy Spirit and He will send Him to us. The promise is, *If you then, being evil, know how to give good gifts to your children, how much more will* your *heavenly Father give the Holy Spirit to those who ask Him!*

Love Overflowed:

My understanding of the Holy Spirit has expanded; the meaning and importance of the Holy Spirit's indwelling as God's deposit of love and His desire to have us with Him is reassuring and brings security. Thank you Father for the reminder and promise that Jesus will come to redeem us—take us home with Him. Until then, my prayer will be as Jesus spoke:

saying, "Father, if it is Your will, take this cup away from Me; nevertheless not My will, but Yours, be done."—Luke 22:42.

Have you invited the Holy Spirit to fill your life? Do it now. Ask God to fulfill the promise above in Luke 11:13 for you and those you love. God's gift is the deposit of the Spirit.

Be so full that even if they take and take and take and take, you can still be overflowing.

—Alison Malee

But you shall receive power when the Holy Spirit has come upon you; and you shall be witnesses to Me ...
—Acts 1:8

Divine Appointments

This morning my husband and I were up early to leave for appointments over an hour and a half away. I read a couple of devotional thoughts and scriptures as we were traveling. We had prayer together. I prayed that God would give us some divine appointments and help us encourage others for Him today.

After the first appointment we treated ourselves and went out to breakfast. Then we went to the church and caught up on some pending items. Two hours later I kissed him goodbye and headed to the Subaru dealership. My 2005 Subaru was scheduled for a mandatory recall repair for the airbags. I had originally scheduled it for another day and another time but changed it to this time because of the other appointments on the same day. I wanted to get all our errands done and checked off the list.

After checking in I headed for the waiting room. A gentleman was already settled in. I greeted him and we began chatting about the current world crisis of dealing with Covid-19, the political climate and spiritual implications.

31

As our conversation was progressing, a woman joined us. We caught her up on the discussion and invited her participation. We made rapid advancement in sharing our views and then some personal information.

I had a pile of papers on my lap. I knew my wait was going to be about an hour. So far, I hadn't touched them. She noticed them and said, "Looks like you came prepared to work."

"Actually, I did. I'm writing a book and I'm going through it making some corrections and additions."

That seemed to cause some excitement and she began questioning me. When she found out I was a healthcare chaplain, I learned from her that she worked with handicapped children and hospice patients playing therapeutic music. We continued to reveal more and more about ourselves to each other. All the time we shared, the man was listening intently. He had his own questions.

"If I'm not being too personal, would you mind telling me how you go about publishing a book?"

"I don't mind at all," I responded. I began sharing and gave him several scenarios. He then opened up and trusted us with what was on his heart to write. He said, "I've had this in mind to do for a very long time."

I encouraged him, "I've found that if we have a dream planted deep within our heart that keeps resurfacing, it is usually God Who planted it there." He liked that response and nodded in agreement.

After the lady listened to us for a while she timidly chimed in. "My, this is interesting. I've always wanted to write a book, too. I would call it, *Grace*.

The man said, I think I would entitle my book, _____.

I looked up that title for him and said, "Well, it looks like someone else already thought of that." Then I read the description of the book. It sounded just like what he had been sharing. I invited him to add another word or two to his original idea. The lady commented, "It sounds like you have a soul-mate."

There was more sharing. Then something was said that made me think of an experience I had gone through. It was about trusting and calling out to God. They wanted to hear it so I began sharing. Shortly after I started, the serviceman came in and asked for the lady. She looked at him and looked at me and said, "Well, we're in the middle of a story. I want to hear this. Can I ..."

He said, "I only need you for a minute!"

I told her I would put myself on pause and wait for her.

But the minute she left, the man said, "Well finish your story." So I did. I told him I would tell him in case he was called out next and didn't get to hear it, but when she returned I had to tell it over again for her.

We started talking about the love and marvel of God bringing us all together—same interests—same dreams—similar experiences. I laughed and said, "Well maybe God brought me here to encourage the two of you to get with it and start writing." They both felt there was a truth in that.

The man said, "Who would have thought that I would be sitting here hoping they'd find something else wrong with my car so I don't have to leave?"

So shall My word be that goes forth from My mouth; It shall not return to Me void, But it shall accomplish what I please, And it shall prosper in the thing for which I sent it.—Isaiah 55:11.

Three of us sat in the service waiting room at the Subaru dealership amazed at God. Have you ever been in awe of God when you are part of how He has orchestrated events that include you? God had divine appointments prearranged for the three of us there.

With Love Overflowing

My one-hour appointment turned into over two hours. God kept me there until they both had gone. When I retrieved my car I found they had taken care of another problem my car had—no charge—and had checked out a few other things, giving me recommendations and prices.

If we are willing, God will use us and speak through us to challenge and encourage others. While I was busy sharing Jesus, His love, His interest in us and His desires for us to use our talents for His glory, Jesus was busy blessing all three of us individually—drawing us each closer to Him, and providing for my needs with my car.

Three strangers. One room. A loving God Who smiled down on us and spoke to our hearts, reminding us that He knows who we are. He has a plan for each of us. He delights in bringing His children together. He thrills when we share stories about Him and enjoys watching His plans unravel for the good of all. The wonder of God's divine appointments— appointments set up two weeks previously.

Love Overflowed:

God's divine appointments. He ordained this time for His children to get together so that the dreams He had placed in their hearts could be realized and encouraged for fulfill- ment. In His love, He desires that our joy be full and that we live life more abundantly.

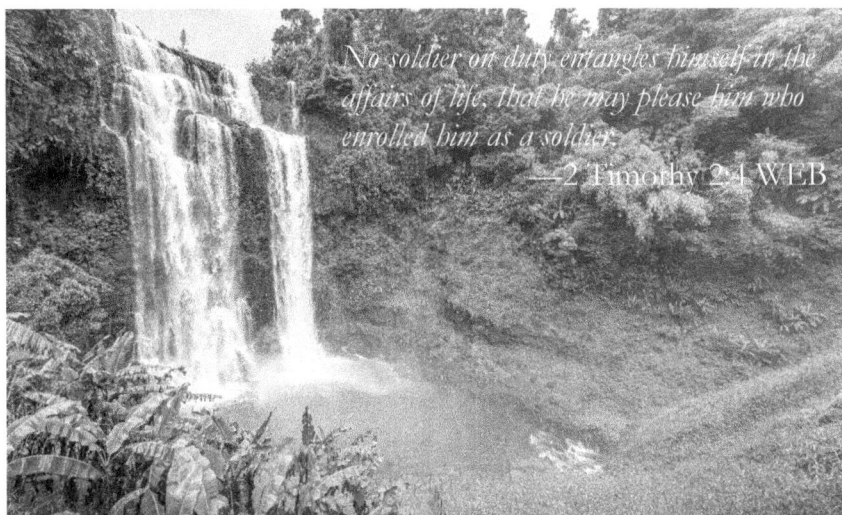

No soldier on duty entangles himself in the affairs of life; that he may please him who enrolled him as a soldier.
—2 Timothy 2:4 WEB

Excess Baggage

Is it our age, our metabolism, our love for food or maybe all three? Have you been struggling to get those unwanted pounds off, without much result? Carrying this excess baggage is uncomfortable and has a negative effect on our health and agility.

Or maybe it isn't our weight so much that is bogging us down and keeping us from enjoying life to the full. Maybe it's the "baggage" we drag with us everywhere we go that's keeping us from making any significant progress.

I would like to suggest that those bags are full of our life's "garbage." If we open up that bag—whew—it stinks! Garbage stinks! Today I want to invite you to dump it in the trash, or "leave it behind."

There is "excess baggage" that we carry around—knowingly or unknowingly. That's the burden of unforgiveness. In one of our other stories we talked about David—who the Bible tells us became King David. Interestingly he addressed things with a different attitude than God addressed them. When he had enemies, he cried out to God to punish them, get even, destroy them.

With Love Overflowing

Jesus instructs us in Luke 6:27-28 to deal with our enemies another way. He says, *But I say to you who hear: Love your enemies, do good to those who hate you, bless those who curse you, and pray for those who spitefully use you.* The key words there are "love," "bless" and "pray for."

When we do things God's way, we have freedom—and peace. The load is lifted. No more excess baggage. No more burden to bear.

I encourage you today to face your unforgiveness issues. Give it to Jesus, but do what He instructs. Ask Him to help you "love with His love and forgive with His forgiveness." Then open your Bible to Luke 6:27-28 and claim the promise. Start blessing and praying over the one who has offended you. Lighten your load today and exchange it for peace and joy.

We need to do something about this. Follow Colossians 3:13, *bearing with one another, and forgiving one another, if anyone has a complaint against another; even as Christ forgave you, so you also* must do. Why **must** we forgive? Because God tells us specifically in Matthew 6:14-15, *For if you forgive men their trespasses, your heavenly Father will also forgive you. But if you do not forgive men their trespasses, neither will your Father forgive your trespasses.*

I have no intention of letting some "jerk" keep me out of the Kingdom. I would rather get even with them by forgiving them than let them control my life and keep me in bondage.

Sin in our life can also become excess baggage; a weight that we don't need to carry around. John 10:10 tells us, *The thief does not come except to steal, and to kill, and to destroy. I have come that they may have life, and that they may have it more abundantly.*

There is penalty for sin. But the Bible has an answer for that in 1 John 3:5, *And you know that He was manifested to take away our sins, and in Him there is no sin.* Once again our excess baggage is removed by accepting Jesus gift to us. We need to take action on this, trust our Savior and release our sins—

asking forgiveness for them and let Jesus transforming love penetrate our heart.

For God so [greatly] loved and dearly prized the world, that He [even] gave His [One and] only begotten Son, so that whoever believes and trusts in Him [as Savior] shall not perish, but have eternal life. For God did not send the Son into the world to judge and condemn the world [that is, to initiate the final judgment of the world], but that the world might be saved through Him. Whoever believes and has decided to trust in Him [as personal Savior and Lord] is not judge [for this one, there is no judgment, no rejection, no condemnation]; but the one who does not believe [and has decided to reject Him as personal Savior and Lord] is judged already [that one has been convicted and sentenced], because he has not believed and trusted on the name of the [One and] only begotten Son of God [the One who is truly unique, the only One of His kind, the One who alone can save him].—John 3:16-18 AMP.

… Behold! The Lamb of God who takes away the sin of the world!
—John 1:29.

If we want to be well and truly ready for the Lord's return, we have to deal with our forgiveness issues and repent. Take heart that, *The LORD will fight for you, and you have only to be silent.* (Exodus 14:14 ESV.)

Love Overflowed:

Thank You Jesus that You have a way for us to lay down our excess baggage and live a richer fuller life with You in control. Thank You for Your sacrificial love for us, so great that You have already paid the price of our sins so that we can rejoice and move forward in a renewed life—a life of new beginnings.

Is your back tired from carrying around excess baggage? Are you ready to lay your burden down? What do you need to do to move forward unencumbered?

Come to Me, all you *who labor and are heavy laden, and I will give you rest. Take My yoke upon you and learn from Me, for I am gentle and lowly in heart, and you will find rest for your souls. For My yoke is easy and My burden is light.*—Matthew 11:28-30.

The steadfast love of the LORD *never ceases, his mercies never come to an end; they are new every morning; great is thy faithfulness. "The* LORD *is my portion," says my soul, "therefore I will hope in him."*
—Lamentations 3:22-24 RSV.

And He loves me despite the fact I fail Him every day.
—Derry Tannariello

Exploring The Caves

We had come to Arkansas for a very special celebration. It was not only our grandson Samuel's thirteenth birthday, but also the day he had chosen to be baptized—publicly testifying of his love of Jesus and his commitment to follow the Lord's will and purpose for his life.

It had been a very long time since we had seen our grandsons. We looked forward to, not only rejoicing with Samuel, but also spending some quality time with Seth and Simon. They would be staying with us in the bungalow we rented not far from their home.

With their dad, my son Matthew, we checked out points of interest that were nearby. We found a lot of advertisement about the caves there. That had appeal. None of us had visited them before so we anticipated a good time. I didn't know what to expect but I soon found out.

As I was having my devotional study time before we left, our planned day's activities of visiting a cave made me think of David in the Bible. I remembered his story of having to flee from King Saul and hide in a cave. There were those who were loyal to him that fled with him. 1 Samuel 22:1-2,

With Love Overflowing

David therefore departed from there and escaped to the cave of Adullam. And when his brothers and all his father's house heard it, *they went down there to him. And everyone* who was *in distress, everyone who* was *in debt, and everyone* who was *discontented gathered to him. So he became captain over them. And there were about four hundred men with him.*

I thought, what a dilemma. How very uncomfortable. How did they survive for so long? I felt sorry for David and his 400 men, living in a dark, damp, dingy cave.

That was before I went exploring the cave that day with my husband, son Matthew, and grandsons Seth, Samuel, and Simon.

I was enamored by the vastness of the cave and the temperature.

There we were in this controlled environment—perfectly comfortable temperature, pure clean running water down the side of the rock—large flat plateaus convenient for conversation areas, cooking tables or beds. All you needed was something to provide light.

Hmmm, I didn't feel so sorry for David and his men anymore. If over 400 lived there—that was some cave! All they would have needed were some torches, cooking utensils and bedding. Somehow I had pictured him hiding in something more resembling a lion or bear den. But not so. Quite a setup.

Just before the return of Jesus there will again be a time of persecution of Christians that will be seeking shelter in caves. Hebrews 11:38 says, *[men] of whom the world was not worthy. They wandered in deserts and mountains,* in *dens and caves of the earth.* My prayer would be that those that have to hide then will be able to find a cave as vast and inviting as the one we visited.

When Jesus returns there will be another group of people that will be looking for a cave to get away from Him; trying to hide from His presence. Isaiah 2:19-21 says, *They shall go into the holes of the rocks, And into the caves of the earth, From the terror of the LORD And the glory of His majesty, When He arises to shake the earth mightily. In that day a man will cast away his idols of silver And his idols of gold, Which they made,* each *for himself to worship, To the moles and bats, To go into the clefts of the rocks, And into the crags of the rugged rocks, From the terror of the LORD And the glory of His majesty, When He arises to shake the earth mightily.* The wicked will run from Him. The righteous will rejoice.

We had an interesting and exciting day with our family exploring the cave. It also proved to enlighten our perspective on God's provision for His children. God will make a way when there is no other way. He already knows where each of us will be at the close of earth's history and He is able—more than able to keep us from the wrath of the enemy.

Love Overflowed:

By exploring the caves we enjoyed another remarkable display of Your loving provision revealed. Thank You Father that we have nothing to fear unless we forget where You have led us in the past. Thank You that we are secure in You.

For we do not wrestle against flesh and blood, but against principalities, against powers, against the rulers of the darkness of this age, against spiritual hosts *of wickedness in the heavenly* places.
—Ephesians 6:12.

Father, recapture our first love of You and help us to be ready in that day to see You face to face. In Jesus' name, Amen.

Choose this day Whom you will serve. Release all your anxieties to Jesus and exchange them for peace.

With Love Overflowing

Talk It Over With God
—Helen Steiner Rice[†]

You're worried and troubled about everything,
Wondering and fearing what tomorrow will bring—
You long to tell someone for you feel so alone,
But your friends are all burdened with cares of their own—
There is only one place and only ONE FRIEND
Who is never too busy and you can always depend
That HE will be waiting with arms open wide
To hear all your troubles that you came to confide—
For the heavenly Father will always be there
When you seek HIM and find HIM at THE ALTAR of PRAYER.

©Greg Olsen[‡]

[†]©1975 Helen Steiner Rice Foundation Fund, LLC, a wholly owned subsidiary of Cincinatti Museum Center

[‡]©Greg Olsen. By arrangement with Greg Olsen Art, Inc. For information on artwork by Greg Olsen please visit www.GregOlsen.com

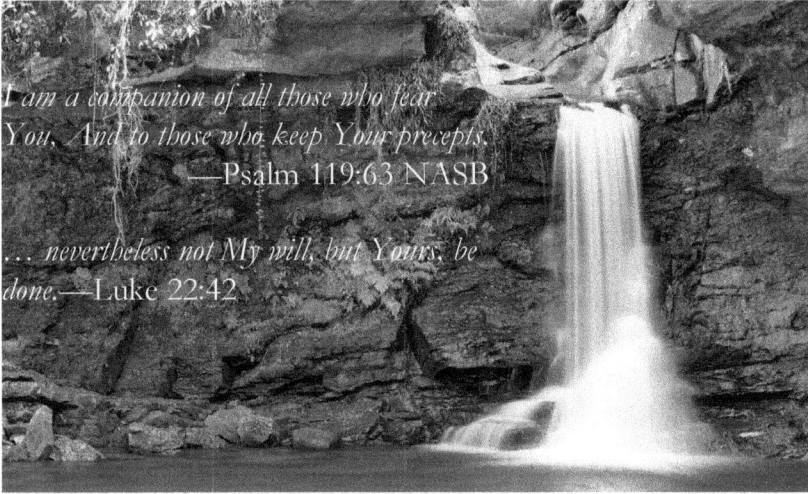

I am a companion of all those who fear You, And to those who keep Your precepts.
—Psalm 119:63 NASB

... nevertheless not My will, but Yours, be done.—Luke 22:42

Facing Foreclosure

My husband had been out of work for some time with a concussion. We were now on the verge of losing our first new home that we had worked and saved so hard to buy. I was receiving foreclosure notices, past-due bills, demands for payment, collection notices and phone calls; "When are you going to pay your electric bill? You have ten days and then we're turning it off."

I was so devastated with all the calls from the bill collectors, and the realization we were so close to having the water turned off, I went to my mother's to wash my hair. I was afraid they would turn off the water once I had soaped up and I wouldn't be able to rinse out the shampoo. I realized if God didn't help us, we could lose our home.

From the time I had become a Christian and had learned the importance of paying a tithe to God, a tenth of our income, God had always provided, blessed us, and helped us through difficult situations. I believed He would again. We had been faithful and His promises says in Malachi 3:10, *"Bring all the tithes into the storehouse, That there may be food in My house, And try Me now in this," Says the LORD of hosts, "If I will not open for you the windows of heaven And pour out for you* such *blessing That* there

43

will *not* be room *enough* to receive it." I was a new Christian; I had not yet learned how to pray the Prayer of Commitment, the "If it is Thy will" prayer. This promise specifically invites us to "try" Him—"test" Him.

Back then, as a new Christian, even though God had proven His promises and the fulfillment of them to me over and over, I still had a terrible problem with worry. The whole situation seemed overwhelming to me. Some days I would cry for hours as I contemplated the future. We had been in a state of foreclosure for nine months. Generally they try to remove you from the house after about six months if you haven't paid your house payment. Needless to say, I was distraught. I cried out to God, "God, save us. God, do something. God, sell the house or help us win a contest with a big monetary payout. Help us do something to pay off the bills."

We had two little boys to care for and there was no money coming in. If we lost our home, or even sold it, where could we move that we could even afford? Everywhere I looked, that we could afford, was worst than I would have imagined. I thought, "How am I going to raise my boys in this environment?" I was worried and frightened. The future seemed so bleak and uninviting. I didn't understand that all my foreboding could be set free with just a moment of genuine praying. Asking God to do 'according to His will,' would have saved so many tears.

God was persevering with me. One day as I was lying on my bed sobbing my heart out, I cried, "Father, I'm not getting up off of this bed until you put a smile on my face." At that moment, after nine months of struggling with this, it was like a light bulb went on in my head. My conversation with God went something like this:

"Derry, why are you crying?"

"Lord, You know why I'm crying."

"Derry, why are you crying? You haven't lost your home yet."

44

"Oh I know, but …"

Suddenly I realized, what God was saying to me was, "the end of the story has not yet been told. Why are you wasting all this time and all this energy crying all the time? If you end up losing your house then you deserve a good cry. If you don't, look at all the energy you've wasted."

From that moment on, my perspective of life changed. I realized how foolish I had been. There's no need to borrow trouble from tomorrow. If it didn't turn out the way I hoped it would, then cry. I would deserve a good cry.

From then on I have been relatively free of worry. God knows the end of a story. Waiting can be trying, but when you know your Father loves you, you are assured He will only allow what is ultimately best for you and yours. His word assures us in Psalm 34:17, The righteous *cry out, and the LORD hears, And delivers them out of all their troubles.*

The rest of the story: No we didn't lose our house. The Lord sold our house, paid up all our bills and gave us enough money to start over. Praise the Lord. He even made it fun for us. He tipped us off that a buyer was on the way, and let us know how much the buyer was going to offer for the house. We were prepared even before the buyer got there. The buyer ended up being a neighbor of a neighbor who called us.

Love Overflowed:

God promises us if we faithfully give back to Him, He will open the windows of heaven. He had other plans for us and had to get us to move. We were facing foreclosure but we ended up in ministry in Northern California and made wonderful new friends. In His love, He wanted to bless us, but we had to be inconvenienced before that could happen.

And we know that all things work together for good to those who love God, …—Romans 8:28.

With Love Overflowing

Are you facing financial distress? What will you do?

Lightning bugs are a lot like Christians. God re-created us with an innate ability to be light in a dark world. Some of our lights flash continuously, while some of our lights tend to be on the blink or not functioning at all.

SOMETHING TO THINK ABOUT: FIREFLIES FOR JESUS

Matthew 5:16 says, [*Let your light so shine before men, that they may see your good works and glorify your Father in heaven.*] We are all called to be lightning bugs, fireflies for Jesus, as the magnificence of His presence shines through our very lives.

Ray Sanders,
The Baptist Messenger

You are the light of the world ... let your good deeds shine out for all to see, so that everyone will praise your heavenly Father.—Matthew 5:14,16 NLT

Fireflies

It was a balmy fall evening. We were enjoying guests out on the patio at our camp home. We had come back from a pleasant boat ride out on the lake and were just settling in for a bite of supper.

Two of the children were warming by the campfire. The other two joined us at the table where a small lantern hung above us casting a soft glow over the table.

Our house is nestled amidst a grove of trees on both sides. The trees towered over the house. Sitting in the back yard the trees in the front were visible over the rooftop.

Night was settling in and we began stargazing. I didn't have my distance glasses on but from where I sat, at first, I thought I was looking at stars through the bare branches from the front yard trees.

I was squinting as I studied them. They seemed bright and close.

As I sat trying to scrutinize the stars, I heard, "Look at that. Are those fireflies?"

Fireflies!!! That's what I was looking at. I was excited. We called to the children and we all rushed out to the front.

With Love Overflowing

The tree sparkled. We all stood there in awe. We had never seen anything like this. It looked like the tree was overtaken by fireflies. We looked across to the other side and saw another tree that appeared to also be full of fireflies. We heard voices so we excitedly called out, "Do you see the fireflies?" There was indistinguishable chatter and laughter.

It seemed like other neighbors at the campground were out enjoying this spectacle.

Another neighbor came out and we called to him. "Look at the fireflies! If you turn off your porch light you will be able to see them better." I was so excited! How could this be? There were so many...but they seemed to be only in those two trees. Were they migrating? Do they migrate? I didn't know. I just knew that I was in awe and so thankful we hadn't missed them. I was so glad our friend pointed them out.

I had just finished calling out to more neighbors to come look at the fireflies when one of the children came up to me and whispered, "They're not fireflies. It's one of those projected lights."

When she quietly shared that with me, I was momentarily confused. Everyone thought they were fireflies!

I looked around and sure enough, she was right. I could see the streaks of spotted light also flickering on the garbage pail next door. I was crushed. How could we have been so deceived? How was I so sucked in by one person's pronouncement of what we were seeing? I wanted to believe it, so I simply accepted what was said. I didn't question. I didn't investigate for myself. I didn't try to reason things out. I simply believed.

This whole experience was very revealing to me. It made me think of what the Bible teaches us about how satan will come like an angel of light to deceive us.

And no wonder! For Satan himself transforms himself into an angel of light.—2 Corinthians 11:14.

48

Satan disguises himself to appear good instead of evil. Too often we are taken in by his lies and convinced that evil is good and good is evil. It can be difficult to "sort out." Sometimes he will present something to us that we really want to be true or real and we just accept it…hook, line and sinker. He can be very convincing. He wants us to think he knows best and his way is better…more fun.

Jesus is coming soon. He does not want us to be deceived. We are to watch, wait and study to show ourselves approved. There will be many false teachers that could lead us astray. We need to know what is truth. We need to be aware of the devils tactics so we won't get pulled in to his schemes.

There was another thought that came to me from the fireflies…this one is more positive. Jesus is called the light of the world. We are to be a light shining for Him.

Let your light so shine before men, that they may see your good works and glorify your Father in heaven.—Matthew 5:16.

We can be a light to those in darkness. We are told not to hide our light under a bushel in Matthew 5:14-15 RSV, *You are the light of the world. A city set on a hill cannot be hid. Nor do men light a lamp and put it under a bushel, but on a stand, and it gives light to all in the house.*

Jesus doesn't want us to hide our love for Him or our faith in Him. He doesn't want us to conceal our talents or abilities but to use them for the good of the kingdom of God, to make a difference for good with our fellowman.

Love Overflowed:

Father, Your creation is so magnificent! It was exciting to think that we had been invaded by your critters. It was even more revealing to find how easy it is for us to fall into a trap of deception. What gentle, tender love; and what a fun way for You to warn us to be on guard … to be alert to the wiles of the enemy—through fireflies. Thank You. In Jesus' name, Amen.

Will you heed the warning of this story and be on guard so you can avoid being deceived? Don't take anyone else's word for it—check things out for yourself. Better yet, check things out with God. Remember the fireflies!

If you are willing and obedient, You shall eat the good of the land. —Isaiah 1:19

You crown the year with Your goodness, And Your paths drip with abundance. —Psalm 65:11

Gleaning Apricots

When I was younger and had a house full of children, we used to do a lot of canning and preserving. It was time that I found enjoyable and rewarding. Once the house became an "empty nest" I did infrequent canning because I didn't need to stockpile like I had when there were so many mouths to feed; but when I did, I still found it pleasurable. Sometimes I missed doing it. I reflect, with a deep sense of satisfaction and appreciation, on the family bantering and camaraderie that resulted from our efforts to preserve fresh-picked produce and restock our pantry.

The importance and blessing of canning and filling the pantry with good quality food was passed down to my children, so when I visited my son Nathan and his family in Canada and found that was one of the activities scheduled, I was delighted.

Apricots were in season and they were ripe and ready for processing—but first we needed to harvest them. We piled in the truck and headed for the orchard! We were allowed to glean from the crop, mostly going for the ones that had

With Love Overflowing

dropped on the ground. No problem there. The ground was covered. These would be the ripest and sweetest!

We all grouped together and received our buckets. Nathan gave us instructions. We were to fill up our buckets and then empty them into larger five gallon buckets that would then be transferred to the back of the pickup truck. The harvest would be plentiful. We were looking forward to a good and productive day.

The LORD your God will make you abound in all the work of your hand, in the fruit of your body, in the increase of your livestock, and in the produce of your land for good. For the LORD will again rejoice over you for good as He rejoiced over your fathers,—Deuteronomy 30:9.

The pickup we were to load our bounty in was a "new" old pickup that had just been added to the family. My grandson Benjamin, then about six, was quite enamored with it. "This is our new truck Grandma. You have to see what it can do." He was more excited about the truck than picking apricots—that was apparent and understandable.

52

Once receiving our buckets we all headed off to fill them—including my three and a half year old granddaughter Talitha.

She became very diligent and quickly filled her little bucket and dumped her apricots into the larger bucket. Then back at it again!

Benjamin on the other hand was enjoying a stroll. His walk in circles always took him back to the same place—the truck.

Pretty soon he was in the truck checking it out again; admiring all its knobs and handles.

Papa Nathan tracked Benjamin down and encouraged him to do his part. Benjamin picked up his bucket and started filling it—but didn't get far. He wandered off again ... to the truck! For a young boy who enjoyed mechanical things, it was just too difficult to stay away. The desire to investigate and figure out how things work and what they can do is just a wonderful part of Benjamin's nature, even today.

With Love Overflowing

After this happened a few times, his papa pressed the point, reminding him that he enjoyed eating them but wasn't doing his part. That appeal didn't last long. The next coaxing included consequences if he didn't participate.

Talitha, who had been consistent in her contribution, had her bucket almost full again. She heard her papa's warning to Benjamin. Benjamin was now working—ever so slowly.

Talitha took note of the consequences Benjamin would encounter and she quietly and slowly made her way to where Benjamin was, still dawdling. No one was looking—except Grandma, on the sly. Talitha, without a word, dumped her little bucket of apricots into Benjamin's and took off to refill hers again.

Talitha's actions made me think of how love looks out for one another. Love is aware. Love cares. Love finds a way. Love puts others first. Talitha is still consistently finding ways to show love and caring.

Let nothing be done through selfish ambition or conceit, but in lowliness of mind let each esteem others better than himself. Let each of you look out not only for his own interests, but also for the interests of others. Let this mind be in you which was also in Christ Jesus,
—Philippians 2:3-5.

Love Overflowed:

Gleaning apricots gave me a different perspective of my grandchildren. How inspiring to see that at three years old this Jesus quality of love had already been instilled in my granddaughter. I wonder how many of us, much older and considered wiser, have yet to learn the important lesson of how to love unselfishly?

Each individual is given the opportunity to help bring light to a world struggling to find its way in the swirl of darkness.
Author unknown,
1992 Prayer Journal, Birth

Who comes first with you—yourself or others? Is Christ's character of unselfish love being perfected and exemplified in your life?

If not, today would be a good day to repent and ask for Jesus' help in recognizing the needs of those around you and the opportunity to share His love.

The Joy Of Unselfish Giving

—Helen Steiner Rice[†]

Time is not measured by the years that you live
But by the deeds that you do and the joy that you give—
And each day as it comes brings a chance to each one
To love to the fullest, leaving nothing undone
That would brighten the life or lighten the load
Of some weary traveler lost on life's road—
So what does it matter how long we may live
If as long as we live we unselfishly give.

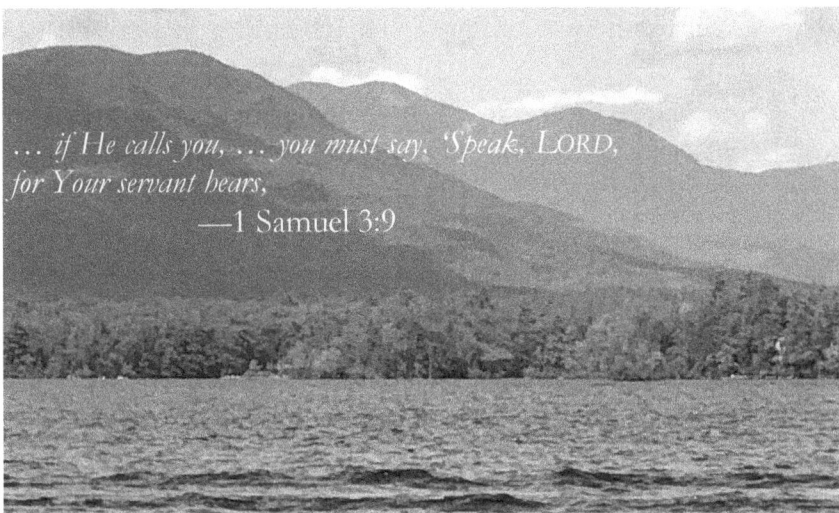

... if He calls you, ... you must say, 'Speak, LORD, for Your servant hears,'
—1 Samuel 3:9

God Sent Me Back

A few hours after dark we were still on the road. We were in a hurry to get to our destination. Weather was moving in on us. We stopped at a gas station to refuel. I told my husband I would be right back. I needed to use their facility. He asked me to please hurry.

I ran inside to use the Ladies room and ran right back out the door. As I left the Lord spoke to me and said, "You didn't even speak to the girl in there." (There was a young lady behind the counter. No one else was there.)

Perplexed, I responded, "No I didn't, Lord. I was in a hurry to get back to the car."

Then I heard, "Go back in there."

I thought, *Really??? Like what am I going to say?* But I have learned it doesn't do any good to argue with God so I went back.

I came in and smiled at her and apologized, "I'm sorry. I just ran in here and ran right back out. I didn't even acknowledge your presence. How are you?

"Fine," she responded with a quizzical look.

With Love Overflowing

"Well is there anything I can remember in prayer for you tonight?"

She began to cry and said, "Oh yes. Please. I was on duty here last night and a gunman came in and held me up at gunpoint. I'm so scared!"

I remembered Isaiah 26:3: *You will keep* him *in perfect peace,* Whose *mind* is *stayed* on You, *Because he trusts in You.* I shared encouragement and assurance of God's love and protection; then we prayed.

WOW. Thank you Jesus for loving her so much that you would use me to go in and pray for her and reassure her of Your love and watch care. Your love understands what it is like to be in a violent environment and face danger.

the LORD *will watch over your coming and going both now and forevermore.*—Psalm 121:8 NIV.

Father, I want to hear You more and walk in Your empowerment. I want to know Your heart, be quick to obey, do Your will, and bring You joy. Please fill me, use me, overflow through me to Your children. Pour forth Your love through me in ways that will draw others to You. In Jesus' name, Amen.

Love Overflowed:

God shows up in the unlikeliest places. God sent me back and used me to calm this young woman's fear and reassure her that He was watching over her with His protective love. Deuteronomy 31:6 says, *Be strong and of good courage, do not fear nor be afraid of them; for the* LORD *your God, He is the One who goes with you. He will not leave you nor forsake you.*

Will you be ready to encourage someone today? What fears do you need to face? Are you willing to replace them with something that can bring you courage and peace? The promise in 2 Timothy 1:7 assures us, *For God has not given us a spirit of fear, but of power and of love and of a sound mind.*

58

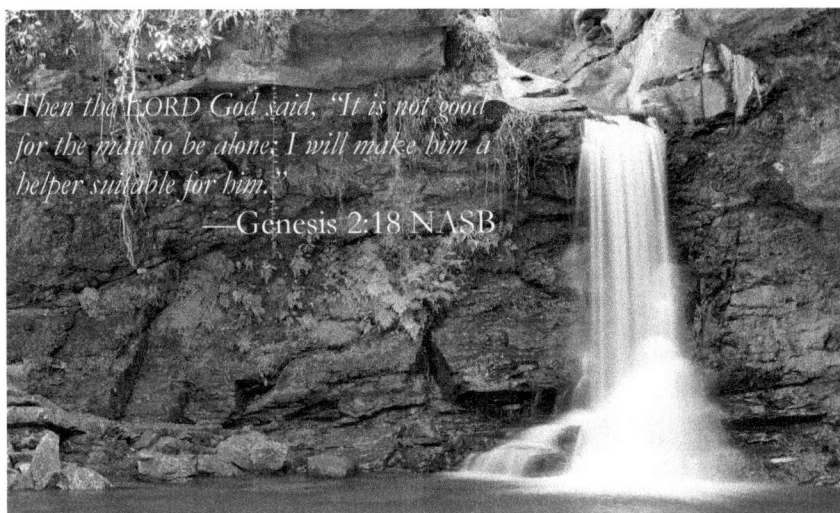
Then the LORD God said, "It is not good for the man to be alone; I will make him a helper suitable for him."
—Genesis 2:18 NASB

God's Gift—My Husband

It was the weekend. I decided I was going to stay home from church and just spend the time with God. I did a lot of reading and felt led to read the story of Isaac and Rebekah. I learned a number of lessons from the story and contemplated them with God. I was inspired. At the close of study time, God gave me the scripture in Genesis 12:1-3 ESV, *Now the LORD said to Abram* (Derry), *"Go from your country and your kindred and your father's house to the land that I will show you. And I will make of you a great nation, and I will bless you and make your name great, so that you will be a blessing. I will bless those who bless you, and him who dishonors you I will curse, and in you all the families of the earth shall be blessed."*

That verse was like a stab in my heart. You know when God is talking to you. I actually gasped. And thought "Oh no. I love it here." A few days before I had said, "God, I love it here. I am so happy I could die here. Nevertheless, if You want to give this place to someone else, if you have something else in mind for me, Your will be done. That's where I want to be." I also said, "I know You indicated previously that You had a companion in mind for me; but I'm almost at the point where I'm not much interested anymore. I'm rather enjoying it being just You and me. If that's what You really have in mind, I think we better be getting on with it, because I'm not very open any more."

The next day I was cleaning the house. I had praise music on and I was singing my heart out with it. Suddenly, I stopped in the middle of the hallway, with dust rag in my hand raised toward heaven, jovially stated with the appropriate accent, "Father, I think that what I need is a good Italian man!" Then I went back to cleaning.

I had been alone nearly 12 years. I enjoyed my job as Manager of Chaplain Services at our community hospital and had a very special staff of volunteers. We all shared concern for one another's challenges and unmet needs. A number of them felt it was time for me to get serious about having a companion. They had been praying for some time about God sending me the right person. My son Geoffrey had recently instructed that if I ever got married again, I should marry an Italian man with daughters so he could finally have sisters.

On this particular day, one of my chaplain volunteers came into my office to have a heart to heart talk with me. She had been praying that morning and had sensed that God was prompting her to encourage me to go on eharmony in search of the perfect companion. I couldn't help but laugh. My immediate reaction was, "Well if God wanted me to do that, He could have told me Himself. Besides, I had someone talk me into on-line dating a number of years ago. No way! It was awful. I woke up the following morning with hundreds of hits from desperate men. It was disgusting! After all of her hard work setting me up, I immediately removed myself from that site. I'm too old fashioned for that. God can orchestrate our meeting. Why, He can even bring him here to my office. Wouldn't that be just great?"

She had made a special trip in to give me the news. She wasn't even on duty that day. Unable to convince me, she got up to leave. As she was almost to the door, the scheduled volunteer came in. We were all close friends as well as co-workers. Before I could even say "hello," she said, "Derry, during worship this morning it was strong on my heart that you need to go on eharmony and fill out a form."

"What? You guys have both lost it. I'm not doing any such thing. Besides, God hasn't told *me* to do that."

The following week I was scheduled to be out of the office to attend a conference. On my return flight home I had a two-hour layover. Reading is a hobby of mine so I headed for the bookstore at the terminal. I had so many books at home that I hadn't read yet, I had no intention of buying any more. I was just looking and killing time. As I surveyed the shelves, a book all but flew into my hands, *How to Find Your True Love in 30 Days or Less.* I laughed "Oh, right." In amusement, I began to browse through it. I opened it to a section that said something like, "Most Christians think that God will bring their true love right to their door, and He can. He can also use the computer." Oh no!!! I slammed the book shut and started to put it back on the shelf when I heard a little prompting in my heart... look through it. Reluctantly, I took the book back down and opened it.

When I opened the book up again I was at a section giving instructions, such as:

- If you do go on-line and join eharmony or Christian Match, fill out every question.

- Check your on-site mail daily or those matched to you will think you aren't really serious about wanting someone in your life, or they may think you have already found someone.

- Fill in every place for pictures. Put in pictures of you doing various things you enjoy and depict who you are.

- Don't hide anything. You want to be loved and accepted for who you really are.

With Love Overflowing

I groaned and closed the book. This was too much.

I had to go to work as soon as I returned home. I was tired from the trip and had jet lag. The day seemed to drag. Finally off duty, I headed home ready for a quick meal and then some relaxation. Generally, I rarely turned on the television, but this night I grabbed a plate of food, sat down on the sofa, put my feet up, turned it on and hoped there would be something descent to watch for a few minutes. I offered a silent prayer asking God to help me find something acceptable I could watch while I ate so I could just veg a few minutes.

I couldn't believe my eyes. As soon as I turned the TV on, a commercial for eharmony came on. "Join eharmony— Free weekend. Join now." "Okay God, this is the third time. I will do it, but I'm not happy about it."

After dinner I headed upstairs, with an attitude, and began filling out the questionnaire for eharmony. I followed all the instructions I had read in that blasted book at the airport. I filled in every picture. Pictures of me looking good, overweight, having fun and preaching! I figured that would discourage a man. This time, I also listed all my degrees, hoping they would leave me alone because they would feel intimidated.

The following day I sat down at the computer and prayed before I opened eharmony to review the results. I closed out over 155 interests. I kept two potentials and responded to them.

From the beginning, one gentleman really piqued my interest. After corresponding back and forth a few times, he had my attention. Each time I got on the computer, before I communicated with anyone, I spent time in prayer. If this is really God's plan, I didn't want to miss His gift ... and I also didn't want my own way.

It was amusing to me how God answered my prayer. He impressed me with some very witty things to say, words I knew I was unable to have come up with on my own. And they worked. The gentleman I was most interested in turned his head, took another look at my profile and continued to pursue more information.

We soon were on the phone talking. He had a great voice. He was fun and interesting to converse with, however getting our schedules to jibe was a bit complicated as I was on the west coast and he was on the east coast.

On our third call he shared, "I just want you to know that I have been on this dating site for a while. I had my list narrowed down to three women who are all very interesting to me. I think any one of the three would make a good companion. They are serious potentials. I had no intention of looking for anyone else and then you showed up. I decided to keep it to three, so I have replaced one of them with you." I started laughing and said something cute. He took the bait and hung on.

Several more weeks went by. He let me know that he was at the place in his friendship with the other gals that it was time for him to meet them. Okay, that was fine with me. I was of the mind that I wanted only who God wanted for me. God knew where I could best serve Him and win others to His heart. God knew everything about both of us. He knew whether Ron and I would complement each other, whether or not we were compatible, and most importantly, whether or not we would bless God in our ministry together. Besides, I wasn't emotionally tied to this guy yet anyway—but was very intrigued.

On Tuesday I received copies of a DVD that had been made of the annual Pastors Appreciation Banquet I had hosted as Chaplain of the hospital. The event was video recorded so it could be aired locally to show how our spiritual leaders were working together for the good of the community. I was highlighted because I was the hostess, MC, part of a skit, and sang with our entertainer.

With Love Overflowing

When I got home I sat the DVDs down on the desk. I heard God say, "Send one to Ron." Stunned, I responded "No way. You've got to be kidding. That's like marketing myself. I'm not going to do that." Again I heard, "Send one to Ron." I sat down and put my head in my hands and prayed. After praying, it came to me, "Why not? It shows exactly who I am. It shows me preaching, praying, serving, sharing, and being spontaneously fun as I responded to our entertainer's invitation to join him singing a song. If Ron doesn't like what he sees, it's better to know now and not carry this friendship any further. Okay Lord, I'll send it." Thursday morning I dropped it in the mail. The postmaster assured me it should arrive on the east coast by Wednesday the following week. Ron lived in New Hampshire and I lived in California.

During our Friday evening phone call, Ron shared that he would be leaving the following morning to meet one of the ladies he had been communicating with. He said he would be flying out at 5am to Nashville, Tennessee and asked if I would please pray for him. I said, "Of course. I was contemplating fasting this weekend. Now I will fast for sure and will cover you with prayer." Then I asked him if he would like for me to pray for him before we hung up.

As I was praying, words came forth asking that God would reveal any secrets, both positive and negative about this lady, and that after Ron left from visiting her, he would know for absolutely sure whether she was the one God intended for him to spend his future with. That was also the focus of my prayers when I fasted that weekend.

Before Ron hung up he said, "By the way, I'm watching the DVD you sent. It's pretty entertaining. My dad loves it." How could he have it already? I just mailed it the day before. It had to have been carried on the wings of angels. There is no way it could have gotten from one coast to the other in one day!

64

On Saturday, from the time I woke up, Ron was on my mind and God began showing me scripture promises to intercede for him. Once I started praying, I seemed not to be able to stop. God kept pouring into me and I kept interceding. I got out of bed a couple of times to get a drink or use the bathroom; otherwise I was in God's Word and in prayer. Periodically, I sensed an urgency to pray in a specific way.

Around 8:45pm my time, 10:45 where Ron was, I suddenly felt released from any need to pray. I smiled and thanked God. Then with a chuckle, I said, "You know God, Ron promised he would call on Monday when he returned home and let me know how everything went. Now, I can wait until Monday, but it sure would be fun to hear from him before that; especially if he already knows whether she is the one."

Within 15 minutes, the phone rang. It was Ron. I was excited and thought this must mean he had rejected her as a choice. Then I listened to his report. "She's terrific," he said. "Everyone here loves her. We had so much fun, we forgot to eat. She was going to fix me a meal, but it got so late that we ended up going out. We've been on a walk. She showed me where she works. I met a number of her friends. She is just lovely."

As he was sharing, I was praying. I said, "Thank you Lord. I was really starting to get interested but had a number of questions in my heart. I know You alone know who You have in mind for me and that is what I want. Not my will but Yours." A bit disappointed, but trusting God, I responded, "Ron, I am so happy for you. It sounds like God has answered our prayers. It sounds like you will be leaving there with no question about her."

He said, "Absolutely! I can't wait to meet you. I don't want to wait until Fall. I want to meet you this Spring. In fact, I want to come out in a couple of weeks. Will that be alright?"

I actually took the phone away from my ear and looked at it, and said "What?" He had had a great time. She was wonderful. He wants to meet me? "What?" Then he said, "I do know for sure, Derry. She is not the right one for me." I was floored. Off balance, I didn't know whether to feel relieved or apprehensive. We ended the call with a tentative time for him to fly out.

Something that Ron was unaware of was that a few years previous to our meeting, God had taken me on a shopping trip to Michael's, where He let me know what I was to purchase. At God's direction, in the cart went netting in three different colors, purple, a lovely green and soft mauve, almost pink. There were other items that matched the netting, some silk flowers and complementary accessories.

I began to laugh, and said, "Father, it looks like we are getting ready for a wedding. If this is for me, wouldn't it be nice if I had a 'groom' and gave him the privilege of discussing his choice of colors for the wedding?"

God just said, "Trust Me."

"Okay, I guess I will know he is the right one if he chooses the colors we have here," I jokingly laughed, so I purchased the items and put them in a box in my garage. For the next few years, God kept adding to my stash. Occasionally, I would say something like, "Well Father, we have the table decorations for the reception, the decorations for the church, I guess I will know when we are getting close when You either bring the groom or show me my dress and the bridesmaids' dresses.

Every now and then I would take time to glance through a catalog that had arrived in the mail to see if there were any dresses in the colors of the netting. Nothing. The green was hard to match and so was the purple. Until … I returned from a trip and started sorting out piles of mail and an abundant supply of catalogs.

I began piling the catalogs up to toss them out when God distinctly told me to pick one back up. When I opened it up, it opened to a page where the dress shown matched the green netting. I turned the page. There was another dress in exactly the right purple. They were on sale for $39.99 and $45.00. I just sat there and looked at them. They were nice enough. Yes, they might just work; but who were my bridesmaids? What sizes would I need and how many did I need to order? When I checked the size chart I found that both dresses came in small, medium and large. That was unusual. I asked God how many I should order. Answer: "14." "You've got to be kidding! What sizes and what colors?"

Information in hand, I picked up the phone to place my order. The person on the other end of the line said, "Since you are getting so many, we will give you 15% off and free shipping." Can you imagine? I got 14 dresses for just barely over $500. I thanked God for the good deal and said, "I'm sure You'll let me know who these are for when I need to know.

Now we just needed my dress and the groom. "Looks like we are getting closer and it appears as though when this happens it is going to happen pretty fast," I thought. Dresses arrived and were boxed up and placed in the garage with everything else. Still waiting.

Unexpectedly and unintentionally, one day not long after that, I was out shopping for a dress to wear to a party and found my wedding dress. When I got it home I realized that the sleeves of the wedding dress were just like the sleeves of the bridesmaid dresses already stored. Hmmm, now all we need is the groom.

It was only a few months later that this whole computer dating business came up. Now I was looking forward to meeting Ron and felt released to let my heart really warm to him.

I was nervous and excited when I arrived at the airport to meet him. When I saw him come down the escalator with his jacket swung over his shoulder, I thought, "Hmmm, cool hand Luke." When we first came together we giggled and I said, "You're just the right size." He put his arm around me and gave me a hug and said, "Yes, I am."

A few weeks prior to his due date, I asked him if he would be willing to meet some of my friends at lunch on the way back from the airport. He looked forward to it. I didn't tell him how many. I figured that since he was a pastor and dad of four daughters, he ought to be able to handle it. I invited over 20 of my girlfriends to size him up. I was anxious to see how this would go. We were meeting at a Chinese buffet. At that time I had no idea that a Chinese buffet was one of Ron's favorite places to go.

All things considered, it went relatively well ... nerves aside. It was unanimously in his favor. The girls approved. I was being cautious, scrutinizing, but enjoying myself.

It was later that evening and the next day that the field of red flags grew. Trained as a chaplain and one who taught classes on how to deal with grief and loss, I had some knowledge and experience in assisting hurting people. Having lost his wife from cancer, I realized Ron had a long way to go yet in his grieving process. I could see that this guy was nowhere near ready to be in a serious relationship or even think of marriage. That could be well documented by him insisting that we look at some 2000 pictures he had on his computer. Most of them were of his past wife. "See, there is her head in the water. We were at the lake." After hours of sitting and looking through his pictures, I was worn out and very concerned.

The next day, I walked in to him talking to one of his daughters. I could hear her yelling at him, "Dad, what are you doing?" He was crying, "I will never love anyone but your mother." Wow, I had heard enough. Go back home. I cooled quickly. From then on, I just watched the clock.

Fast forward: Ron went home. We kept talking. Talked through what happened when he was in California. I went to Canada to help my son and daughter-in-law after the birth of my granddaughter. Ron called while I was there. We were growing closer. Months went by. He came out for another visit. On the way back to the airport, he said, "Can we talk hypothetically? If we were to get married ..." He had a number of questions. I held my breath.

After answering each one I said, "Okay, hypothetically, if we *were* to get married, what colors would you want in the wedding?"

He was thinking the guys. "What do you mean, either black or white?"

"I mean for the girls to wear, for accent colors, flowers."

"Oh I don't know. What about purple, green and pink?" I began to cry. Those colors just rolled off his tongue. All three. First answer. No hesitation. "Seriously God, this is the one? Really? I'm still not so sure." Of course I knew that the devil also knew the colors so I wasn't yet convinced. I still had a number of questions as to why God would have me marry this man. We had some divergent faith issues that had

69

me question this union. I had been trusting God from the beginning. I would continue to wait upon Him.

Come July, I headed to New Hampshire to meet his family. They're not ready for this either, but somehow God has a plan and God's plans will not be thwarted. Against my own better judgment, but in obedience to God's direction, wedding plans were on. There were still issues to resolve. I needed a replacement at work; a new manager over Chaplain Services and I needed to do something with my home.

I had serious reservations about Ron being ready to get married, but God had made it clear that he was the one. I spent time in prayer. I simply surrendered to His will. I promised Him that if this was His plan, I would also abide by His timing. I simply said, "Lord, I will know it is Your time when You replace me at work and have someone for the house. You have made me steward over Your house and I will not leave it unattended. When you send someone to rent, lease or buy, when You turn the house over to someone else, I will know it is Your time." Honestly, I figured that would buy me quite a bit of time. But not so ....

That weekend, as I was attending a local seminar, a woman whom I had not seen in maybe five years came up to me. "I can't believe you're here Derry. Just this week God told me that I needed to talk to you."

"Well I *am* here. What do you need to talk to me about?" I responded.

Hesitantly, she stammered, "I don't even know how to say this. Last week God told me that I was supposed to ask you for your house. I don't even know what that means. I have no money. I can't afford to buy it. But I believe I am supposed to start a ministry in it."

"When are you supposed to do this?" I asked.

"As soon as possible, I believe," she countered.

Within two short weeks, God had the position at the hospital filled and had a new "caretaker" in *His* house.

70

In August, eight of my treasured pastor friends participated in our wedding. The closing remark of one of the pastors was, "I've never been at a wedding where the Holy Spirit was so present." The Lord let me know who to ask to be bridesmaids. All the dresses were the right sizes.

Today, I thank God that I let Him do the choosing and I continue to rejoice in the revealing of God's plan for us individually, as a couple and in ministry. Scripture (Ecclesiastes 4:9 KJV) says, *Two are better than one; because they have a good reward for their labour.*

Life doesn't always happen as we wish or expect. Our situation may look or seem impossible, but God has a plan and destiny for each of us and He knows where we can best be of service to Him. We may not understand His choices or leading, but we can trust that His ultimate goal is for us to spend eternity with Him. Trust His perspective and surrender to His will. Put your love for Jesus above any other love.

Love Overflowed:

Thank You Father that Your ways are not our ways. You see what I cannot, and know what is best for me and how and where I can most win others to you. Thank You for this man You have chosen for me—Your gift, my husband, and for our families. Help me to be all that he needs and all that You want me to be in this relationship that we might serve You in ministry as a dynamic duo. May this love that You have lavished on us pour through us to love others to You. I love and trust You Jesus, in Your name, Amen.

who has saved us and called us with a holy calling, not according to our works, but according to His own purpose and grace which was given to us in Christ Jesus before time began,— 2 Timothy 1:9

If you have questions about the relationship you are in—talk to Jesus! He has a divine plan that is for your eternal

With Love Overflowing

best. If you are alone, reach out to someone else. He can direct you to the right person. If you are with someone, He can heal, restore or make it even better. We all need each other. Won't you take a minute and commit your relationship to Him now?

May the Lord make your love increase and overflow for each other and for everyone else, just as ours does for you.
                    Ryan Callahan

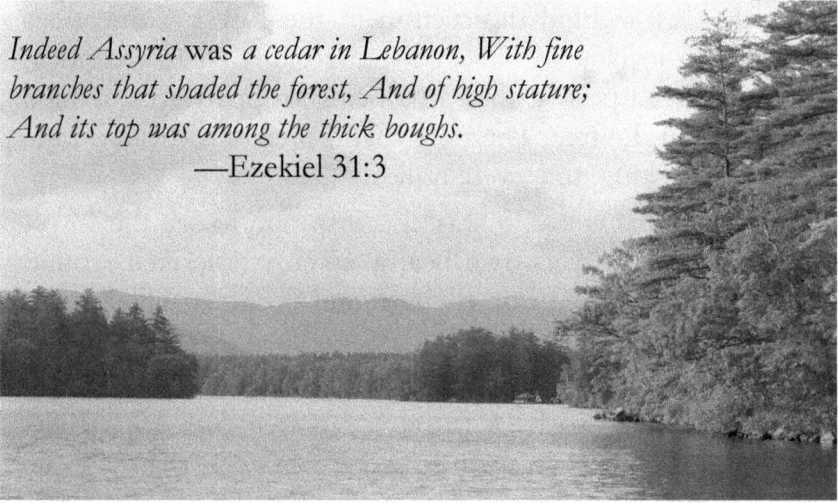

Indeed Assyria was a cedar in Lebanon, With fine branches that shaded the forest, And of high stature; And its top was among the thick boughs.
            —Ezekiel 31:3

Hiding In The Redwoods

If you have never been to the Redwoods in northern California, it is difficult to describe the majestic appearance of these towering giants. Just to stand in the midst of them is overwhelming. You are captivated by their strength and grandeur. But they have also suffered, as did the cedars of Lebanon mentioned in scripture—Zechariah 11:1-2, *Open your doors, O Lebanon, That fire may devour your cedars. Wail, O cypress, for the cedar has fallen, Because the mighty* trees *are ruined. Wail, O oaks of Bashan, For the thick forest has come down.*

Interestingly, redwoods can live through drought. Their leaves pull in the moisture from the ocean and the fog. This causes them to rain on the forest floor and bless the other little plants trying to thrive under the protection of their splendor.

Let's apply this to ourselves. Like the redwoods, we can live above the troubles of the world by letting the Holy Spirit rain on us, to water and nourish our soul and spirit, and use us to share encouragement with others.

It is fascinating to be in the deep woods where these giants have continued to stand after surviving a lightening

73

storm that left behind destruction in the forest. Some trees toppled over leaving an over ten-foot stump. There were others that suffered part of their side being stripped off leaving a gaping hole in the tree. The trees that toppled had been on the ground for so long, they were hollow.

While this is sad, it was also inspiring to see the forest restore itself. It held its own beauty when you looked around the destruction to focus on the fern and flora that filled in the decay.

These were the woods that held our interest and repeatedly beckoned us back to pitch our tent and stay awhile. Why? Because, we enjoyed this section for more than just the beauty. It was a wonderful playground. There was usually a significant time spent each day of our vacation utilizing the environment for our pleasure.

1-2-3-4-5-6-7-8-9-10. Here I come, ready or not! Where are you? That was an oft repeated chant heard throughout camp when we were hiding in the Redwoods. We would hide in hollow trees, climb up high stumps that offered inviting ledges to shrink into, or flatten ourselves against the side of open gaps carved out by the lightening.

Sometimes we would hide so well, we couldn't be found. Not because the search stopped, but because we were so well concealed.

Those mighty, captivating trees that held such a commanding presence gave me another insight. Even though they were injured or broken they still served a purpose—they were a great hiding place.

There are times in our lives when we are injured and broken, and feel we have no purpose. We have no one to confide in. We are not alone, though we may feel like we are, as did King David in Psalm 69:20, *Reproach has broken my heart, And I am full of heaviness; I looked for someone to take pity, but there was none; And for comforters, but I found none.* We have hopes and dreams, but it seems that everything in our life, our present circumstances contradict them.

Sometimes we couldn't be found when we were playing Hide and Seek, but there is One Who always knew where we were—our Jesus. We can't hide from Him. He is omnipresent—with us wherever we are. It is also reassuring to know that in our brokenness we can call out to Him and *He heals the brokenhearted And binds up their wounds.* (Psalm 147:3.)

With Love Overflowing

He assures us that He has a plan for each of us in Jeremiah 29:11, *For I know the thoughts that I think toward you, says the* LORD, *thoughts of peace and not of evil, to give you a future and a hope.*

Love Overflowed:

Thank You Father that there in the forest, hiding in the Redwoods, we encountered Your presence. You said to Israel, *I will be ... like a refreshing dew from heaven. ...* (Hosea 14:5 NLT.) In Your healing presence of boundless love we are refreshed and invigorated, inspired and restored.

The righteous shall flourish like a palm tree, He shall grow like a cedar in Lebanon.—Psalm 92:12.

Stop playing hide and seek and come rest awhile in the Presence of God and ask Him to refresh, revitalize and strengthen you. Don't wait. Do it now.

Have you not known? Have you not heard? The everlasting God, the LORD, *The Creator of the ends of the earth, Neither faints nor is weary. His understanding is unsearchable. He gives power to the weak, And to* those who have *no might He increases strength.*—Isaiah 40:28-29.

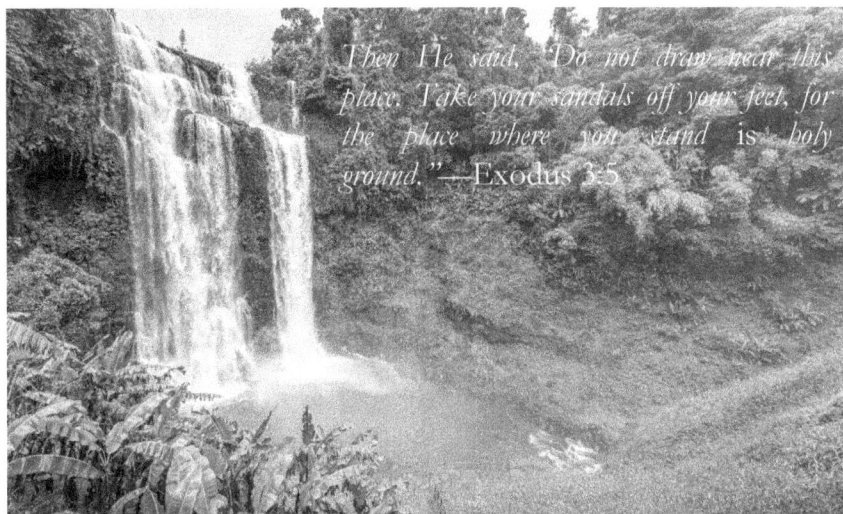

Then He said, "Do not draw near this place. Take your sandals off your feet, for the place where you stand is holy ground."—Exodus 3:5

Holy Ground

When I worked at the hospital in California, I developed some friendships that were very dear to me. I had a couple of very faithful volunteers whose spiritual background was in eastern and western religion. Besides believing in Jesus they also had a guru. This was a bit unusual for me. I had not heard of this belief before.

One day I was invited to attend a wedding at their chapel. When I arrived, to my surprise, I saw shoes piled outside the entrance doors to the chapel. I, in turn, took mine off and set them aside. Looking to the front as I entered I could see there was a picture of Jesus on one side and a picture of their guru on the other side.

As I sat down I was thinking about the shoes at the door. Were the shoes removed out of respect for both Jesus and their guru, or out of respect for the "presence" in the chapel? I wasn't sure, but what did come to my mind was the scripture above from Acts 7:33, *Then the LORD said to him, "Take your sandals off your feet, for the place where you stand is holy ground."*

With Love Overflowing

I thought wherever God is, is holy ground. If He asks us to remove our sandals/shoes because He is present, why aren't we doing that? Here I am at a chapel where they do remove their shoes. If they can for their guru, shouldn't I be doing it for my God?

Now when I go into church I remove my shoes. Why? Because I'm expecting God to show up and where God is, is holy ground. I want the power of the living, victorious God, name above all names God, to enter, to be welcome, to know that respect reigns and His holiness desired. I want to experience His glory.

I have to admit my practice has prompted some strange reactions. My husband was once asked why he couldn't afford to buy me shoes. He responded, "Shhh, she's walking on holy ground."

Love Overflowed:

What a testimony of respect this was to me. My awe and respect for God was aroused and now a gesture of my love and honor involves removing my shoes in the sanctuary for my Lord and Savior—whether I am sitting as part of the congregation or speaking up front.

Then the Commander of the LORD's army said to Joshua, "Take your sandal off your foot, for the place where you stand is holy." And Joshua did so.—Joshua 5:15.

There are three places in scripture where God meets one of His children and instructs them to take off their shoes because they are on holy ground—standing before Him. Taking off one's shoes is a sign of reverence, humility and respect. Our God, Who gave all because of His love for us, surely deserves that.

How do you express your love, honor and respect?

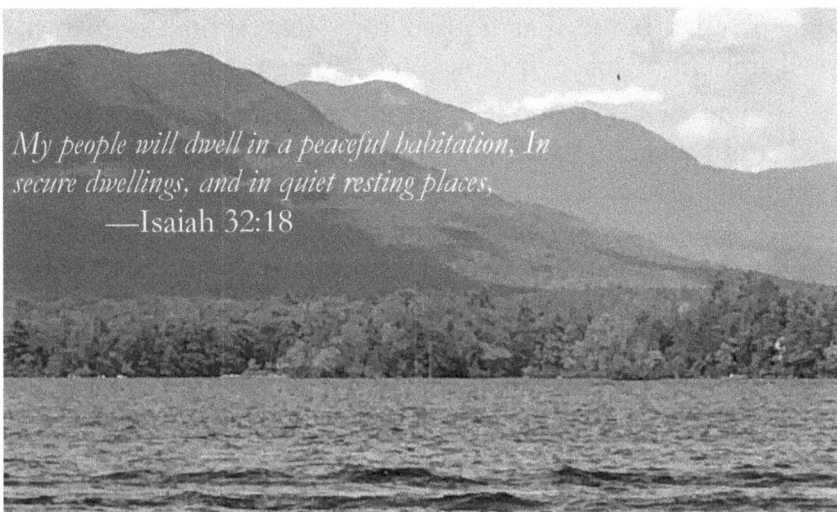

Home With A Mountain View

There comes a time when the children are grown and you know it's time to make some changes—changes like downsizing where you live. We had been talking about it for years and we had finally come to the decision that we better start looking for another place. We just wanted a small place near a lake where we could take out our kayaks, go boating, swimming or fishing; a quiet, peaceful place.

Our daughter-in-love Jamie came across a place she thought sounded interesting. We followed her lead and made an appointment to look things over. It was a campground re-sort condo across the street from a sprawling, crystal clear lake. The lake itself is a relatively quiet lake where you can enjoy nature wherever you are on it. It is not buzzing with towns or shopping around the shoreline, just the beauty of trees and the sounds of nature.

When we toured the campground we found each site had an RV Model home with an extra room attached. The total square footage of each home is 550 and you are allowed to put up a small storage unit on your lot. It was hard to imagine going from a home that housed four generations to such a small amount of space. It took some getting used to.

The first few models we looked at were older, very used, and packed! I couldn't even envision living in them even though the outside areas were rather inviting. One had a small stream next to it. Another had a small but pleasant patio area and was located across the road from the pool and play area. The campground also had a lodge with a workout room and another out building with an indoor pool and hot tub. Several laundry rooms and shower facilities were located throughout.

When the owner of the resort finished showing us around and what was for sale, I asked, "Do you know of any others that might be coming up for sale?" As a matter of fact he did. We were unable to go inside but he said he had heard talk that they might be on the market in a few months.

Once again, I asked, "Is there anything else you know of?" My husband looked at me quizzically.

The response: "Well, I know my parents will be putting their place up for sale at some point, but probably not for a couple of years yet."

"May we see it?" I surprised myself by asking. (I wondered at my forwardness.)

"I can show it to you from the outside. I don't have the keys with me to let you in. It will probably be a long time before they are ready to let go of it." he stated.

"Okay, I get that."

By now my husband was becoming a little annoyed at me and tried to excuse us by interjecting, "We don't need to waste his time, Derry. If the place isn't available, it's not available."

Fortunately the owner placated me and started driving over to his parent's site. You might guess, I had been silently praying about this whole thing, asking God if He even wanted us in this area.

We arrived at the site and the moment my foot touched the walkway my heart heard God say, "This is where you are going to live." I said nothing. I just looked around the outside.

It had a large brick patio area and a pleasant local view of the mountains. It was surrounded by trees and flower beds all along the walk and surrounding the two-level patio area. Hidden around the back corner was the storage shed. I just stood and took it all in—silently. Then thanked him profusely for showing us. I told him I thought it was lovely and to be sure and let us know if his parents put it up for sale.

After our first visit, my husband was convinced that he wanted to move there when the house sold. We made another trip back several weeks later to check out other homes that had come up for sale. The last one we looked at caught our eye. It was a beautiful new unit on a site that overlooked a small part of the lake. The drawback for me was that it was directly above the noisy main highway. In the few minutes that we stood out on the very small patio area, the fumes from passing traffic were joining us. Nevertheless, the inside was stunning. It was a terrific floor plan and they had done an exceptional job decorating. My husband made an offer on it.

As we were sitting at the table in negotiations, I again surprised myself by interjecting, "Should we write in the agreement that we have first right of refusal?" Both men, the owner and my husband, looked at me like I had lost my mind. The owner said, "We have never, in all the years of doing business here, had someone agree to sell and then retract it for another offer." Feeling rather foolish, and wondering where that thought had come from, I sat back and said nothing more. The offer was filled out, signed, and a small deposit made—until we knew it was accepted. My husband would then send in a check for the balance of the deposit he was offering—after he had transferred funds. The campground owner expected we would have an answer promptly.

Once in the car my husband asked why I had said that. "I don't know. It just came out of my mouth. But there seem to be a lot of people looking right now. People will put that statement into a contract to protect their right to deal."

True enough, we heard back right away. Our offer was accepted. My husband responded that he would immediately get on the phone and have funds transferred. There would be a check in the mail the following day for the balance of the deposit.

In the meantime, I'm thinking and praying—"Well God, I must not have heard you correctly. I was sure you said we were going to live in that other place. Maybe that's where You want us in a few years—to move there??? I was confused and surprised at the turn of events.

The following week we had not had any further communication regarding the unit we put a deposit on. We were expecting to receive additional papers to sign and a move in date. Finally my husband called the resort owner and queried him. "Ohhh, he replied sheepishly, "the owners sold that unit to the neighbors this weekend for full price."

My husband was stunned! "You've got to be kidding. We had a deal. I mailed in the check."

"No problem. I'll return your check to you."

My husband got off the phone and looked at me with determination. We are going up there tomorrow and pick out a place. That is where we are going to live.

"Sweetheart, the other places we looked at were 'dogs,' old, beat up, packed with junk." I pointed out.

"Well, we are going to have to pick one of them. We need to have a place to move to as soon as the house sells." he stated emphatically.

Gulp! *Oh, no!* I thought. My husband is serious. I started praying—hard. "Father, it sounds like my husband means business. He is determined. If you have in mind for us to live where you showed me or anywhere else, please have it go up for sale by tomorrow morning before we get there."

We called and made an appointment. The next morning we arrived to revisit the models that we had already seen. I waited for the proper formalities and greetings, anxious to ask if anything else had come up for sale. But before I could speak, our new friend said, "Well, you might be interested to know that I received a call from my parents this morning. They have decided to put their place up for sale. My dad is getting too old to make the trip back and forth here and is ready to let go of it."

I was so tickled. I hadn't told my husband the whole story yet. I couldn't wait to go back up to the site and this time go inside. I knew that since the outside was so inviting, the inside would be perfect also. I was right. Because this home had been occupied by the co-owner of the camp, it had extras in it that most models didn't have.

There were extra closets and drawers in the master bedroom area. There was a dishwasher and a stacked washer/dryer unit. It wasn't as new and beautiful as the one we had put the deposit on. It didn't come with the cupboards full of new cookware or nice dinnerware like the other one did, but it had benefits the other one didn't have—mostly the large patio in a quiet cul-de-sac with lovely flower gardens around it and an exhilarating view of the mountains across the lake. We put a deposit down on it and this time it went through.

Several weeks after we had settled in, God sent us a special "kiss from heaven." As we looked out the sliding glass door enjoying the view, we were awed and inspired to see a rainbow suddenly appear. It seemed to be touching our home. To us, another indication that our covenant-keeping God was telling us we were where He wants us to be and that He is abiding with us!

Love Overflowed:

My heart had been troubled about the future and the outcome of what our living situation would be. I could only talk to God about it and trust in His understanding and in-comprehensible love. He always comes through!

I couldn't stop praising God for giving me the fore-knowledge and for the gift of such a peaceful place. Our new seasonal home is bringing us much restoration and revitalization of body, soul and spirit. It's a chosen place given of God where I can sit out on the patio and look out at the mountains and be inspired to write, and write, and write. The fresh air is intoxicating and the atmosphere invigorating. Even in times of uncertainty love produces a heart of gratitude. God of majesty, what a wonderful God and Father You are! Thank You for our home with a mountain view.

And I will establish a place for My people Israel, and will plant them, so that they may live in their own place and not be disturbed again, nor will malicious people oppress them anymore as previously,
—2 Samuel 7:10 NASB.

Do you know where God wants you to live at the close of earth's history? If not, talk to God about it—and your needs. Pray for a passion for God's presence to dwell with you and invite His overflowing love to fill your home.

With Love Overflowing

When Troubles Assail You, God Will Not Fail You
—Helen Steiner Rice[†]

When life seems empty And there's no place to go,
When your heart is troubled And your spirits are low,
When friends seem few And nobody cares
There is always God To hear your prayers—
And whatever you're facing Will seem much less
When you go to God And confide and confess,
For the burden that seems Too heavy to bear
God lifts away On the wings of prayer—
And seen through God's eyes Earthly troubles diminish,
And we're given new strength To face and to finish
Life's daily tasks As they come along
If we pray for strength To keep us strong—
So go to Our Father When troubles assail you
For His grace is sufficient And He'll never fail you.

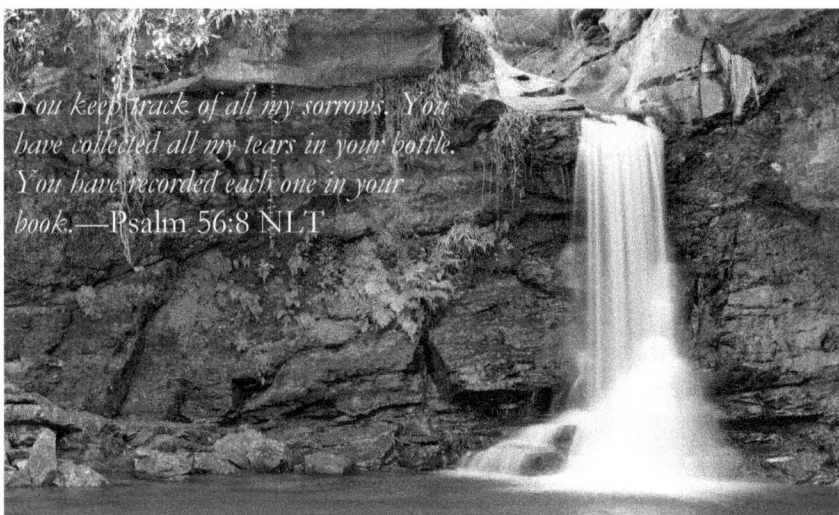

I Do Love You

When I was struggling through the beginning stages of my divorce and my heart was in deep turmoil, I was agonizing over the rejection and betrayal I was experiencing. I felt so alone, abandoned and unloved. With David in Psalm 6:6 NIV, I wept, *I am worn out from my groaning. All night long I flood my bed with weeping and drench my couch with tears.* Truly my pillow was drenched with tears. I wondered how I would make it to work and assume my responsibilities with any sense of sanity.

It was then that God said, "Praise Me."

I choked, "Praise You, God? I can barely speak."

"Praise Me."

Knowing, and having already experienced the truth, that "God inhabits the praises of His people and praise dispels the enemy" I directed my attention to praise. I tried to sing a song of praise. I croaked it out. I tried again. My voice was stronger. Again, stronger, until I was singing with all my heart.

This happened day after day. I would wake up and begin to cry; then praise my way to work. I was reminded of Bible stories where praising armies conquered the enemy and won wars. After I started my day with praise, I did my Chaplaincy and management duties fully present. God used me to bless and encourage others. My ministry at the hospital, by God's grace, was effective and fruitful only because He was faithful to pour Himself out through me as I reached out to bring comfort and encouragement to others.

I would return home, walk in the door, and my grief would overwhelm me again. I would fall apart and cry. This happened day after day for several weeks until one evening after a most distressing phone call from my soon-to-be ex-husband, I went upstairs to the office. My little parakeet was in there. I checked on him. I gave him his food and water and talked to him for a few minutes. Then as a wave of grief overwhelmed me again, I claimed the scripture promise in Psalm 119:76 NIV, *May your unfailing love be my comfort, according to your promise to your servant.*

I fell across the sofa and sobbed, "Jesus, where are You? If only You were right here. If only I could crawl into Your arms. I need to hear You tell me You love me."

I had just finished those words when my little bird, Homer, flew to the side of the cage, hitting it hard, holding onto the wire bars, looking out at me and said clearly, "Jesus loves you."

I was stunned. In utter awe I just watched my bird as he immediately dropped down and began to eat. Just like that. "Jesus loves you." And then back to life as normal!

In the day when I cried out, You answered me, And *made me bold* with *strength in my soul.*—Psalm 138:3.

Homer had only spoken a few words and he had never said that before—or since!

My precious Lord spoke to me in a clear, audible voice and told me He loved me through my bird. Jesus is eager to reveal Himself to us and reassure us of His understanding, compassionate love. He is there for us in the big things as well as the small. He knows the cry of our heart, sometimes answering even before we ask.

Dazed, I got up and pulled myself together. That was the beginning of a turn for me emotionally. I clung to my Savior. I let go my fears. I trusted in the future.

When we face trials, it helps to ask, "What can this accomplish for my good? Do we want to be transformed, sanctified and made holy for Him? That won't happen without growth—growing in Jesus and surrendering to His will. He does not call us to follow Him and then forsake us.

Love Overflowed:

Jesus heard my pain and the cry of my heart and spoke through my parakeet Homer, reassuring me of His love and refilling my empty love tank. O love that will not let me go!

… *Blessed* are you *who weep now, For you shall laugh.*—Luke 6:21.

I encourage you to ask Jesus, "Lord, what is Your love message to me today? Who do You want me to love to You?

When you are at the end of your rope, will you come to Jesus and let Him love and reassure you? He will not fail you. He does love you!

With Love Overflowing

She poured all her love into him
But thus she wasn't enough;
Therefore she walked away
To find a fountain
That was overflowing
Always reciprocating
Her desire to be loved and be love
                — Magnetic Mommy Life

For I know the plans I have for you," declares the LORD, "plans to prosper you and not to harm you, plans to give you hope and a future.
—Jeremiah 29:11 NIV

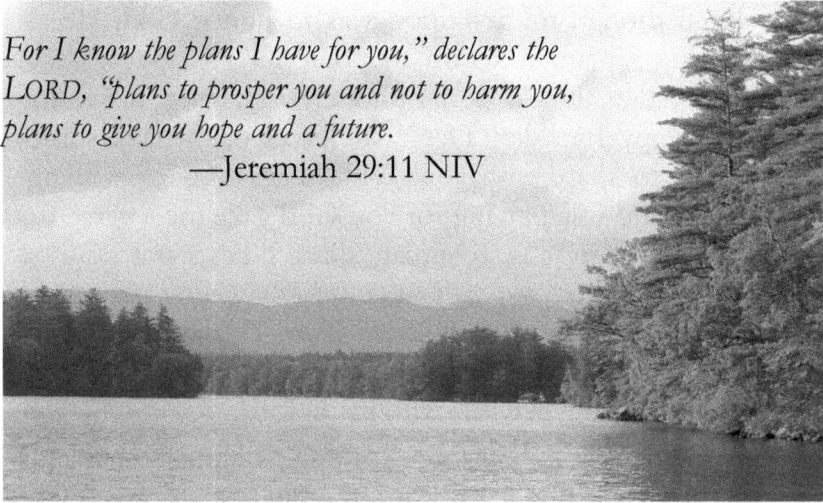

I Know The Plans

It was my birthday. I was living alone and did not have any expectations of celebrating. One thing I have done for many years is give God a gift on my birthday. That means that my gift to God might be to Him directly or in His name and honor I would give something to one of His children. This time I wanted to draw attention to Him "gently". I worked with a number of people who didn't give Him a second thought. I decided to do something a little creative; something I could share that would open opportunities to mention God by Name.

I bought a large birthday cake and purchased some birthday plates and napkins. At work I invited people to stop by for a piece of birthday cake. When they came I thanked them for celebrating with me. I told them I was praising God for the life He had given me and I wanted them to join my praise and celebration of life. This was met with interesting response. It also caused some thought-provoking heart searching in some of my "guests" and gave me opportunity to bless them with prayer.

With Love Overflowing

Even though my intention was to honor God, He already had set a plan in action to pour out His love to me. When I arrived at the office my phone was ringing. It was my mother. "Happy Birthday, Dee," she greeted. "I have something special to share with you. While I was having worship this morning and was praying for you God gave me a verse for your birthday. Here it is, Jeremiah 29:11 NIV, *For I know the plans I have for you," declares the* LORD, *"plans to prosper you and not to harm you, plans to give you hope and a future.* This was very special to me, especially because I could not remember Mother ever sharing anything like this with me before.

About an hour later one of my volunteer chaplains came by the office. She wasn't on duty but she stopped by to wish me happy birthday. Then she said, I have a special birthday text that God gave me for you this morning when I was praying for you, it is *For I know the plans I have for you," declares the* LORD, *"plans to prosper you and not to harm you, plans to give you hope and a future.* (from Jeremiah 29:11 NIV}. Wow, two times God was giving me this gift! Thank you for this promise, Lord.

Before she left, my scheduled volunteer came in for duty. She welcomed me with a big happy birthday greeting and then said, "I'm so excited. God gave me a special scripture for you this morning while I was praying for you. It is found in Jeremiah 29:11 NIV, *For I know the plans I have for you," declares the* LORD, *"plans to prosper you and not to harm you, plans to give you hope and a future.* I was overwhelmed. Usually when God wants to get our attention He often repeats Himself three times. This was the third time ... but not the last.

This gift of promise was followed by another friend dropping by the office with a card for me. When I opened it, the cover read, *"For I know the plans I have for you," declares the* LORD, *"plans to prosper you and not to harm you, plans to give you hope and a future."* I had the card framed and mounted on the wall of my office.

All this happened over 15 years ago. I no longer work at that hospital or have that office, but I do have that framed card hanging in my present office on another wall. A picture that will follow me wherever I go as a reminder that my future is in God's hands and He wants what is good for me.

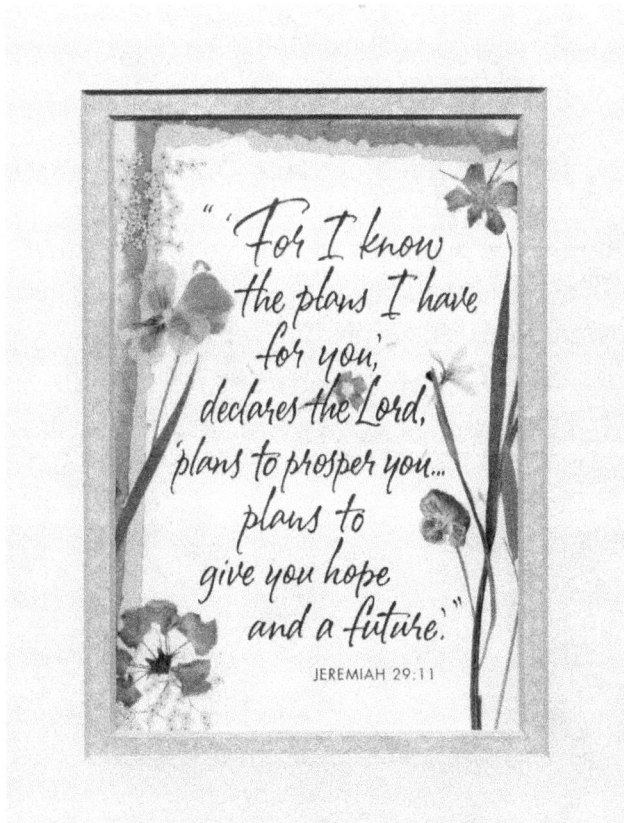

" 'For I know the plans I have for you,' declares the Lord, plans to prosper you... plans to give you hope and a future.' "

JEREMIAH 29:11

Walking with Jesus does not mean our life will be problem-free. In fact, we encounter difficulties because a life sold out to Christ threatens the ruler of darkness and his kingdom of demons. But better to suffer his attacks than live life without the Savior. Our God is the ultimate Victor and He has plans for us that will bring us hope and a future.

With Love Overflowing

Love Overflowed:

Scripture shared from Jeremiah 29:11 carried a bushel full of birthday love to me right from the throne of God. Thank You that no matter how many times I have failed You, Your love never changes.

For God so loved the world that He gave His only begotten Son, that whoever believes in Him should not perish but have everlasting life.
—John 3:16.

Have you been mindful of ways God has reassured you of His love? He has plans for you. He has a myriad ways of getting the message across if we will just be attentive to His presence. It all begins with you!

And He loves us despite the fact we fail Him every day.

We love him, because he first loved us.
—1 John 4:19 KJV

Inexpensive But Powerful

What could be inexpensive but powerful? Are you thinking about it? What would you guess I would be suggesting?

God is Love. In His love He provides for us and gifts us. Some of His most powerful gifts are for us to use in conjunction with Him—our part of building relationship with our Creator and King and building up the Kingdom of God.

I want to propose some inexpensive but powerful ways of knowing God our Father, more intimately. There are a number of ways:

- Prayer—coming in the name of Jesus, Who gives our prayers efficacy.

- A thankful heart—showing God appreciation for all He has done for you. Facing life with a smile.

- Listening to the direction of the Holy Spirit.

- Living a life of forgiveness—asking for it from God and giving it to others…including forgiving yourself.

95

With Love Overflowing

But there is one that is not often mentioned that I would like to home in on here. It is so powerful that armies are conquered and enemies flee. It is so powerful that it can change a heart in a few moments. It is so powerful that walls tumble. I want to tell you, and I want to validate it with scripture. Here it is:

- Praise And Worship—Singing

Now when they began to sing and to praise, the LORD set ambushes against the people of Ammon, Moab, and Mount Seir, who had come against Judah; and they were defeated.—2 Chronicles 20:22.

And when he had consulted with the people, he appointed those who should sing to the LORD, and who should praise the beauty of holiness, as they went out before the army and were saying: "Praise the LORD, For His mercy endures forever."—2 Chronicles 20:21.

God even tells us we can sing praises on our bed and bind up the enemy. This is an honor He has given His saints:

Let the saints be joyful in glory; Let them sing aloud on their beds. Let the high praises of God be in their mouth, And a two-edged sword in their hand, To execute vengeance on the nations, And punishments on the peoples; To bind their kings with chains, And their nobles with fetters of iron; To execute on them the written judgment—This honor have all His saints. Praise the LORD!—Psalm 149:5-9.

And now my head shall be lifted up above my enemies all around me; Therefore I will offer sacrifices of joy in His tabernacle; I will sing, yes, I will sing praises to the LORD.—Psalm 27:6.

Praise elevates us into God's Presence and Power. He will fill our homes and our church.

indeed it came to pass, when the trumpeters and singers were *as one, to make one sound to be heard in praising and thanking the* LORD, *and when they lifted up their voice with the trumpets and cymbals and instruments of music, and praised the* LORD, *saying: "For He is good, For His mercy* endures *forever," that the house, the house of the* LORD, *was filled with a cloud,*—2 Chronicles 5:13.

But You are *holy, Enthroned in the praises of Israel.*—Psalm 22:3.

Whoever offers praise glorifies Me; And to him who orders his *conduct* aright *I will show the salvation of God.*—Psalm 50:23.

Acts 16:25-26 below tells us how Paul and Silas were in jail singing praises to God. Read what happened:

But at midnight Paul and Silas were praying and singing hymns to God, and the prisoners were listening to them. Suddenly there was a great earthquake, so that the foundations of the prison were shaken; and immediately all the doors were opened and everyone's chains were loosed.

They were set free!!!

We are instructed to praise Him, give Him thanks, sing praise, declare His name to those He puts in our life; bless Him. In turn we are promised to be blessed, to walk in the light of God's countenance. All this from a thankful heart that sings!

Therefore by Him let us continually offer the sacrifice of praise to God, that is, the fruit of our *lips, giving thanks to His name.*
    —Hebrews 13:15.

Blessed are *the people who know the joyful sound! They walk, O* LORD, *in the light of Your countenance.*—Psalm 89:15.

saying: "I will declare Your name to My brethren; In the midst of the assembly I will sing praise to You."—Hebrews 2:12.

With Love Overflowing

Enter into His gates with thanksgiving, And into His courts with praise. Be thankful to Him, and bless His name.—Psalm 100:4.

Take note of what the Father is seeking in the following text. He desires that we will worship in the Spirit—the Holy Spirit of truth. Have you heard of the Holy Spirit? The Holy Spirit is part of the Godhead. They are three in one; Father, Son—Jesus and Holy Spirit. All loving us and eager for us to join them in the kingdom for eternity.

But the hour is coming, and now is, when the true worshipers will worship the Father in spirit and truth; for the Father is seeking such to worship Him.—John 4:23.

Love Overflowed:

Doesn't it seem difficult to believe and even explain that there is power in praise? Just like you read in the above verses, what happened in the days of the Bible writers can happen in our lives today. God keeps His word. Maybe not the way we expect, or even hope, but He will. He will always respond in ways that are for the best in our life. Overcoming the devil, overcoming despair, overcoming hopelessness, overcoming rejection, overcoming and winning the trial that you are facing can happen. Maybe it begins with a song—not any song—but a song of praise, thanksgiving and "warfare" where we include the mighty name of Jesus our Loving Savior. There is victory in Jesus!!!

Do you have a song? Will you sing it? God doesn't care whether you can carry a tune. He just wants to hear your voice lifted in praise. I challenge you to step out in faith, open your mouth and praise.

The Bible gives us a beautiful promise in Psalm 30:10-12: *Hear, O LORD, and have mercy on me; LORD, be my helper!" You have turned for me my mourning into dancing; You have put off my sackcloth and clothed me with gladness, To the end that my glory may sing praise to You and not be silent. O LORD my God, I will give thanks to*

98

You forever. If you are in the middle of a battle right now, I encourage you to go on-line and look up the lyrics for any of the following songs. When you do, find a site that sings the song and displays the lyrics so you can sing along. Some great battle songs to get you started are:

- The Battle Belongs to the Lord
- Faith is the Victory
- Victory in Jesus
- Waymaker
- Sound the Battle Cry
- To God Be the Glory

Sing them on your bed; then pray for God to be victorious in the battle you are personally facing. Pray for your family, your community, your church and our nation.

Praise is an inexpensive but powerful weapon that conquers the powers of darkness. Use it—daily—often!

Jesus spoke of rivers of living water which would flood out from our innermost being. So don't pray to be filled. Pray for overflowing!
—Graham Cooke

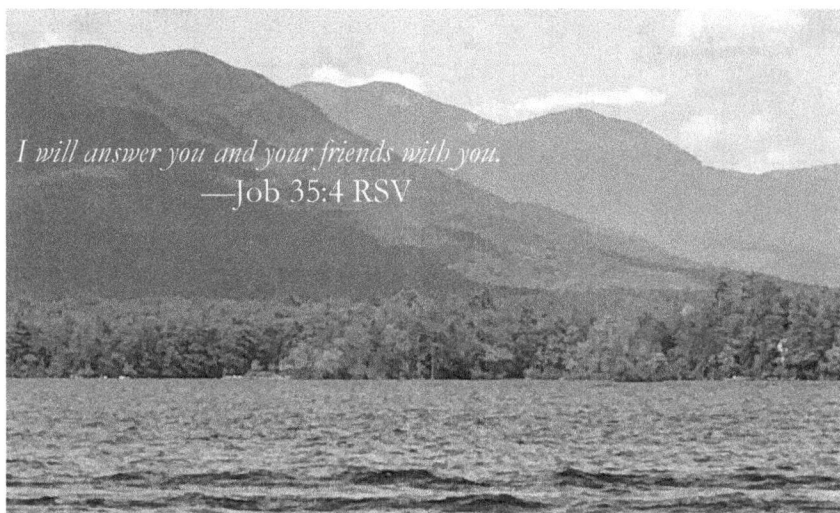

I will answer you and your friends with you.
—Job 35:4 RSV

Just Another Day?

Don't you just love it when God puts you at the right place at the right time? What an exciting moment to find that God has used you to be an answer to someone else's prayer. That's what He did for me yesterday.

My husband and I had been talking about shopping for shoes for over two weeks. We are living in a year-round campground and it's a bit of a trip to go to town. We were both getting pretty desperate for a new pair—part of the soles were pulled loose and other complications with them were becoming unbearable. We had been putting it off because it usually takes us quite a while to find something that will work for our feet. Often we have to go to a number of shoe stores before we find anything. Neither of us was looking forward to this venture.

It was late afternoon. We had a couple of errands to run. When we got in the car I asked my husband if he had a pair of socks in the car in case we decided to shop for shoes when we were in town. We were both wearing sandals and hadn't really planned on shoe shopping in the town where we were headed. He looked at me and paused, then he answered as he opened the car door, "No, I don't." And off he went to get them. Mine had been previously packed in the car.

When we arrived in town, my husband asked if I knew where a shoe store was. I didn't, so I looked it up on the map app on my phone and got an address. If we were going to shop, I needed some heavenly assistance. I began to pray for shoes for both of us … comfortable shoes without having to spend all afternoon at it!

When we arrived a young lady introduced herself and offered us her assistance. We found she had come here from Alaska. This was just a summer job and she would be returning. She had come out here rather unexpectedly and was new to shoe sales but hoped she could help us.

My husband and I both have some particular needs when it comes to shoes. She directed us to the New Balance shoe section. After I tried on a couple pair of shoes, I said, "When you are not so busy, if I have a chance before I leave, I will tell you a story about New Balance shoes."

The place cleared from other patrons and she was repackaging the shoes I had tried on so I began to tell her the following story as it had been told to me:

"It was her birthday. No one remembered. Her heart was broken. She went to her room and cried out to God. She felt so alone and unloved.

As she cried out, she thought she heard a voice speaking softly to her. It was God. He said, "I created you. Get up and celebrate your day; this day of life. Go do something for someone else. Go buy a dozen roses and give them to whom I tell you."

"Oh God, I can't do that," she responded. That would cost about $50. I'm saving my money for a pair of sneakers."

Again, God gently replied, "Go buy a dozen roses and give them to whom I tell you."

So she did. As she gave them out, the responses thrilled her heart. "Oh for me, really? Thank you."

She had one rose left. She looked across the street and saw a hospital. The Lord told her to go in. She went up to the nurse's station, told her story, and asked, "Do you know of a patient that would like to have a rose?"

"I know just the patient," the nurse responded. "Follow me."

She was taken to Carlos' room. When she entered his room, tears came to Carlos eyes. She explained why she was there. Unable to speak English, Carlos' translator shared the story as she told it. Carlos responded with more tears and held the rose tight.

As she left, the translator followed her out the door. "Tell me your story again. Why are you here?" So she repeated it again, from the beginning, including how she had argued with God.

"Do you know what you've done here today? This man is dying. His dying wish was that God would send him a red rose. I knew that when I came in and forgot to bring one. Carlos is dying. He probably will not make it through the day. Don't worry about your sneakers. I am the vice president of New Balance Shoes. You will get your new sneakers. Not just now, but you will have new shoes anytime you need them for the rest of your life."

I was just sharing the story as I heard it told. I have not validated the information so I do not know how true it is, but with us sitting in front of the New Balance shoe section and trying on their shoes, it seemed fitting to share that story.

I had only gotten as far as mentioning that God told the girl to get a dozen red roses when the girl I was sharing the story with interrupted me and said, "You don't even have to finish the story. God sent you here in answer to my prayer. I needed direction on something and He has just told me what I must do through your story." She didn't know there was more God wanted to share with her.

With Love Overflowing

I praised God ... but felt led to finish the story. When I was done she told me someone had died. "I needed to know if I was supposed to take someone flowers."

After I finished the story, I mentioned I was a health-care chaplain by profession, and then we shared a little more.

She stood up and looked at me in wonder and said, "In March, when I was in the hospital, it was a chaplain who spoke words to me that reached my heart and helped me stop drinking. I don't drink anymore."

No one else was in the room. It gave me a chance to have prayer for her, praising God and covering other concerns on her heart.

When we finished praying I got up and walked around the room trying out the pair of shoes I had on. As I was walking, my husband said, "I found a pair. These will work for me."

In turn, I was able to announce, "These will work for me, too." (And they still do. I have them on now as I write.)

Love Overflowed:

An unscheduled shopping trip after waiting well over two weeks and an unexpected encounter for God netted two new pairs of shoes within a short amount of time. Three very happy people parted ... all because God poured out His extraordinary all-inclusive love and blessed us each individually. Thank You Father for orchestrating our shopping trip and arranging our schedule! Thank You for answering her prayer and ours as well. It wasn't "just another day." It was a great day!

Indeed, everything is for your benefit, so that grace, extended through more and more people, may cause thanksgiving to increase to God's glory.
—2 Corinthians 4:15 HCSB.

Do you pray before you go shopping? If not, try it. God promises rewards when we pray (Matthew 6:5-6). I challenge you to put Him first in all things.

Call upon Me in the day of trouble; I will deliver you, and you shall glorify Me.
—Psalm 50:15

Logging Truck Collision Averted

There's power in the name of Jesus. Many Bible stories validate that truth but today I also want to validate it in a way that might surprise you as much as it surprised me.

A gentleman friend of mine was traveling with me from Oregon back down to California. We had both been visiting family and friends there. We had to be at work Monday morning and because of some unexpected circumstances were heading back down to California much later than planned. With stops, the trip would generally take us approximately six to seven hours. We decided to get some snacks, fresh fruit and an extra large sub sandwich to eat along the way so we wouldn't have to take unnecessary detours. And so our trip, packed with adventure, begins!

We had already checked the weather and road conditions before heading home. It looked like we could stay just ahead of the storm.

We had been driving on the freeway about an hour and a half when we came to traffic at a dead stop. We could only assume there had been an accident up ahead. We sat there chatting and laughing … for about 15 minutes when it began to snow … heavily. It came down fast and furious. We became concerned. How long would we be stuck in traffic? How was the rest of the trip going to be now? Would we make it through the snow? After sitting there over two hours, we could hear the children in the car behind us and over a lane screaming and crying and shouting that they were hungry. Mitch and I looked at each other. We had been snacking, saving the sub sandwich for later on in the trip.

I said, "Mitch, I think we can get along on half of this sub. How about it? I'm going to take that family the other half and some of our fruit and nuts." He agreed. That's all I needed. I got out of the car, went over to theirs and shared our food to a very grateful family. Then I took our bags of apples, oranges and cookies and started up and down the lanes of traffic, giving out fruit and cookies. It was fun to see the surprises on peoples' faces and hear their responses of gratitude.

After close to three hours we started moving. In a short time, despite the road conditions we were back up to speed. It was dark now and home was a long way off.

Somehow, I found myself in a group of cars a bit ahead of and separated from the traffic behind us. Then the majority of cars increased the gap between us as they moved forward faster than I was willing to go under the conditions.

Without warning, I hit a patch of ice and my car started spinning across four lanes of traffic. As we spun I saw two logging trucks cresting the top of the hill I had just come over. They were barreling down hard and fast. In seconds they would be upon me. I cried out, "Jesus, help me!"

When in trouble before, I had learned to claim the promise in Acts 2:21 ASV, *And it shall be, that whosoever shall call on the name of the Lord shall be saved.* I'm thankful that was ingrained in my heart.

Suddenly my car was back in a lane and headed down the road at an appropriate speed. There was no doubt Jesus intervened!!! I was ahead of the traffic and the logging trucks passed me on the right. That was close!!! Thank you, Jesus.

We pulled over and put the chains on the tires. Driving with heavy sleet and snow is stressful and very tiring. I was alert and focused. About another hour went by ... then our next adventure.

In my distress I called upon the LORD, *And cried out to my God; He heard my voice from His temple, and my cry came before Him,* even *to His ears.*—Psalm 18:6.

I cried out. He heard me and responded.

Immediately in front of me, a car slid on black ice and went off the right side of the road, stopping in the snow just before going over an incline. Before I could veer away from it, I hit the same patch and slid the same path, headed right for the back end of the car ahead of me. Again I cried out "Jesus." If I hit the car I could push them over the bank. Jesus stopped us two inches from their bumper. We were able to back out and get on the road again. We drove along praising God, thanking Him for His protection.

Still dealing with the storm and getting pretty tired, we realized we would be lucky to get home by 3am. Tomorrow was going to be a long day.

Another hour down the road, the storm seemed to be subsiding. We talked about stopping and removing the chains from the tires. We waited too long! Before we could get to an exit and find a place to safely park and remove the chains, we knew we were in trouble again. This time I didn't call out to Jesus; I said, "Oh no!" We ended up at the side of the road—stuck for two hours with the chains wrapped around the axle, unable to remove them. Finally someone came by and gave us a hand.

We were on our way again … briefly. We must have hit a rock when we pulled over. We now had a flat tire! We pulled off at the next exit. Fortunately, there was a tire shop near the off-ramp. We were first in line—the next morning. But needless to say, with two hours yet to go on our trip, we didn't make it back on time.

One critical factor stuck in my mind as I reflected on our trip home. Both times when I called out to Jesus in my distress and fear, He immediately responded. When I called out in my own frustration, not calling upon Him, I got stuck. It reinforced the truth that there is power in the name of Jesus and He is there when we cry out to Him!

Love Overflowed:

God surrounded us with His protective love, saved our lives and kept us from any injuries. I experienced the fulfillment of God's promise that when we call out to Him—He hears and answers. When I put my hope in Him I have nothing to fear.

He has everything under control—everything—even logging trucks averted!

Be anxious for nothing, but in everything by prayer and supplication, with thanksgiving, let your requests be made known to God;
—Philippians 4:6.

Have you learned of the security in calling out in the name of Jesus? When it's an emergency He doesn't delay!

And God will wipe away every tear from their eyes; there shall be no more death, nor sorrow, nor crying. There shall be no more pain, for the former things have passed away.—Revelation 21:4

Many Tears

My first experience with death was when my little sister Debby died. What a precious little girl she was. She loved playing cowgirl and liked to wear her cowgirl hat. Her face was so sweet shaded by her hat with her bangs just below the brim. She loved Jesus and would carry her Bible around with her wherever she went. She cried if she saw a dead bug. She had such a tender heart.

She came down with the measles and had been suffering with a very bad case of them. Measles turned into pneumonia and an extremely high fever. She was taken to the hospital. Two days later her illness had developed into encephalitis—an inflammation of the brain. She didn't pull through. As a young girl myself, I was stunned and devastated. The last time I saw my sister alive was when she left for the hospital. Her death was extremely difficult for my mother.

Being the oldest child, I felt I needed to be strong for Mom. I kept my feelings inside and didn't deal with them. I loved Debby deeply. It was as though she was my real live dolly. I had fun dressing her up, playing with her hair, and walking to church with her. Her sweet countenance attracted attention and I enjoyed showing her off and urging others to engage her in conversation.

It was only about a year later that my dad was found dead in the bed of his mistress. He was 37 and died of a heart attack. He and my mother were in the middle of a divorce at the time he died. My mother's response to his death was a life-changing experience for me. She showed me by her actions what a true Christian is and how a real Christian should respond to those suffering in heart.

My mother no longer loved my dad, but the woman he was with did. Because the divorce was not yet final, my mother was financially responsible for the funeral arrangements. My mother took both my dad's girlfriend and his mother around with her and let them choose what they wanted for my dad's burial and service.

I was only 14 but it made a deep impression on me. I couldn't believe the compassion and respect my mother showed these women, especially after how my grandmother had treated my mother ever since her marriage to my dad. Even though my parents were married, she had been resentful that my mother hadn't aborted her pregnancies.

With a heart like my mother's, she didn't carry around bitterness or forgiveness issues; that's for sure. Because my mom wasn't suffering emotionally from Dad's death, I was able to let out my feelings; not just my grief over his death but also over my little sister's death. All my pent-up tears came out in a flood, as well as unexpected irrational behavior.

The next death I encountered was my grandmother's; my mother's mother. My next-oldest sister had been caring for her so grandma's death was much more difficult for her. This death did not cause a deep heart reaction in me as she and I were not very close. She had her favorites out of the grand-children, and I wasn't one of them. Once again my mother came through valiantly.

I was by this time learning that death affects each person differently. The relationship you have had with them will determine your response and ability to cope and recover.

After raising seven sons, you look forward to grandchildren. Our first grandchild was a little girl. We were elated! But she only lived five months. She died of SIDS (known as apnea) in her sleep. We grieved as a family. My husband and I were present offering strength and support to our son and daughter-in-love so our feelings were capped.

A few years later I waded through the worse tragedy of my life thus far, the death of our son Brian. He was driving home and went off the road and into a tree. The tree crushed him against the steering wheel. He was 25, good-looking, tender-hearted and loving, calm and discerning, and had a gift for being a peacemaker. Anyone who met Brian immediately became friends with him. He was an absolute delight. His death was a terrible loss.

With Brian's death, I went into a survival mode. I took care of the other children, fixed meals and tended their needs, but sometimes couldn't remember how I had gotten from the living room into the kitchen. Everything was very mechanical for a while. Due to my own grief, I fear I did not comfort my other sons and assist them through the grieving process as much as they needed. I had never been taught how to help others through their grief. It took me several months to really pull myself together. His memory is still often on my mind.

My next loss was that of my husband—through divorce. More heartache, transitions and turmoil. With it I faced the loss of dreams and questioned my value and worth—until I really met Jesus!

Many years went by without having to face any more grief, until we learned that my dear friend, in her 30s with two young daughters, had been diagnosed with cancer. Once diagnosed, time went too quickly. Everyone loved Kelly. Everyone felt like they were her best friend. She had a way about her that brought the sunshine into the room when she arrived. Our hearts broke over the loss of her presence.

The next loss was my stepfather's death. I had already moved out of the house when mom married him, but I soon learned to welcome him into the family and was grateful he was part of us. We never had much time together so it wasn't a particularly close relationship, but I was saddened by his death. It was hard to see my mom going through first the difficult caretaking and then the loss.

A number of years later brought the loss of my husband's dad. After we married I had the privilege of Papa living with us, and of participating in his baptism at 93. He was like the dad I never had since my own biological father had died when I was so young, and my stepfather entered the picture after I left home and had moved away. My heart ached when Papa died. I was traveling when he had his heart attack and could not return in time for the services. I still have moments of grief as I reminisce about our time together. I think of him often and smile remembering the time, love, support and encouragement he poured into me as I adjusted to life with his son, away from my own family. He often reassured me that things would be alright.

Two years ago I lost my mother, who for a season had been my best friend. That was a horrendous death to go through because of all the circumstances. I was living in New Hampshire. Mom and my sisters were in Oregon. My younger sister lived with her then. I had not been informed as to the severity of Mom's condition. I had been saying that I wanted to come visit her but there was always a reason why "now" was not a good time for them. Thankfully, I insisted.

I started pursuing flight arrangements for a month out. During that process I received a call from my sister informing me that if I didn't come soon it might be too late. How could this be? I made immediate arrangements. Her cancer diagnosis

112

had been downplayed to me and I was unaware of her suffering or condition.

I was shocked when I saw her. She barely had enough strength to lift her arm or speak. She was gaunt and thin but had put forth the energy to clean up and get dressed. My sister had combed her hair and had her looking lovely despite her condition. Mom stared at me a lot, then stroked my cheek, and told me I was beautiful.

I responded, "Of course I am. I look just like you." Strangers would comment that we looked like twins or asked us if we were sisters.

My sister, exhausted from caring for her had a routine and knew how things should be done. I tried to relieve her but care was needed that I had not yet learned. My physical condition limited my ability to continually lift mother in and out of bed when she wanted to get up and walk.

I had been trained as a Chaplain, to come along side … not to come in and take over or assume I knew a better way. But since we were caring for our mother, it was difficult to not want to jump in and do more.

I was able to feed her soft food and held back the tears as I saw her struggle to eat it. She only spoke a few words after that and seemed to loose interest in anything or anyone.

I will spare the details of the hell associated with Mom's death. No sleep for days. I thank God for my sons, Matthew and Geoffrey who came to support, encourage, and assist. They loved their grandma and love each other. They stepped in and cared for her, helping lift her to change her position, feeding her and sitting quietly by her side. They were a blessing and their presence helped bring some calm.

We had mother set up in a bed in the living room so we could give her 24-hour care. We would attempt to sleep in the recliners near her. One morning when my sister had gone out to feed the horses, she accidentally left the door open. Within seconds a little bird flew in and landed on my mother's shoulder. I put my finger under it and it hopped on. I put it on a soft cloth and handed it to my mom. She held it in her hand and spoke softly to it. Then before it could take flight in the house and create a chase, I released it outside.

Do you think it was sent as a message from God? Whatever the reason for its arrival, it was an unusual incident. It brought courage, peace and solace with it.

A sadness surfaces in my heart as I write. There is always an emptiness when we consider that someone who knows us—all about us—and understands, loves and accepts us no matter what—is no more. It is like a piece of our heart is torn out. I still often long to "talk things over" with Mom or catch her up on my life. Her words of prophecy over me have helped keep me focused. I regret she is not here to see their fulfillment.

Three months ago we lost my stepson Ron. He was the oldest of my husband's children. He had been a precious gift to me as well. I quickly learned to love him. When we met, he welcomed me with open arms and wanted to know all about me. He was respectful, thoughtful and loving. Whenever we got together he would find a minute to get me aside and ask how everything was going and how I was doing. He knew I had relocated across the continent, was separated from my family and had given up all that was important to me to marry his father. He could see that his father was still grieving the death of his deceased wife of 43 years. Unfortunately our visits were few. We lived in New Hampshire and he in Florida. His death was another personal loss to me and his absence is felt.

Why have I shared this list of losses? Because I want you to know we all have heartache to bear and that I can identify with you if you too have experienced loss. The bereavements in my life have been numerous.

It is how we handle our losses and what we do with our life and the memories created that determine our future. Will we be better people because of what we learned from those we parted with? Will we take the good and incorporate it into our life and learn from the negative or "bad" and determine not to repeat the same mistakes with others? Will we cherish their memory but allow ourselves to move on and let others into our life? Will we be so afraid of hurt and loss again that we will withhold our love and caring? Love is a risk. Jesus took that risk for us. Will we take it for others? The Holy Spirit is the antidote for fear.

Are you harboring anger to God because He allowed someone you love to die? I encourage you to "forgive God" for being God, and allow Him to be Lord of your life. We can't call Him Lord and then go our own way or do our own thing or expect Him to do things "our" way. If He is Lord, we must trust Him.

When I was upset with God, I symbolically drew a line on the floor. When I stood on the left of the line I would raise my fist to heaven and cry out, "God, I just don't get it. I don't understand why You _____. I know God's shoulders are big enough for my questions and my anger.

Then I would step over the line and stand on the right side. I would look up to heaven and say, I know You are God. You have always been there for me. One day when I can look You in the eyes I will ask You all of my "why" questions; but for now, I will let go and let You be God and trust You even through my pain.

If I demand my own way, or argue with His way, I am saying I know best and I am putting myself above God. I choose to trust Him and let my heart be at peace. Isaiah 30:15 assures us *For thus says the Lord GOD, the Holy One of Israel: "In returning and rest you shall be saved; In quietness and confidence shall be your strength." But you would not,*

There is an old saying, "It is better to have loved and lost than never to have loved at all." Always take the risk of loving. It is worth the pain of loss. People struggle over releasing their heart to love—resisting love—either to give it or re-

With Love Overflowing

ceive it. In fact one of the questions most frequently asked on the internet is "What is love?" Jesus gave His disciples this commandment in John 13:34-35 NIV, *A new command I give you: Love one another. As I have loved you, so you must love one another. By this everyone will know that you are my disciples, if you love one another.*

If you really want to know what love is, consider closely the life of Jesus Christ. Then you will know what love is and how it should roll out in your life.

We will each leave a legacy behind. What will yours be? Have we made a difference for good or will our parting be a relief to some? If you are not happy with the legacy that you will leave behind if you were to die tomorrow, then determine in your heart to change that while you have time. Make amends where necessary and leave a trail of love and friendship. Glorify God with the life He has entrusted to you and help others see Who Jesus is by your example.

Your eyes saw my unformed body; all the days ordained for me were written in your book before one of them came to be.—Psalm 139:16 NIV.

Love Overflowed:

Through all my heartache, loss and many tears, God tenderly sent His loving comfort, encouragement and hope for the future. He promises in Psalm 30:11, *You have turned for me my mourning into dancing; You have put off my sackcloth and clothed me with gladness,*

For I am persuaded that neither death nor life, nor angels nor principalities nor powers, nor things present nor things to come, nor height nor depth, nor any other created thing, shall be able to separate us from the love of God which is in Christ Jesus our Lord.—Romans 8:38-39.

God in His wisdom has a destiny for you which no one else can fill. Will you let Him fill it through you? What do you need to change in your life to leave a legacy behind that you will be proud of—a legacy of living out His love?

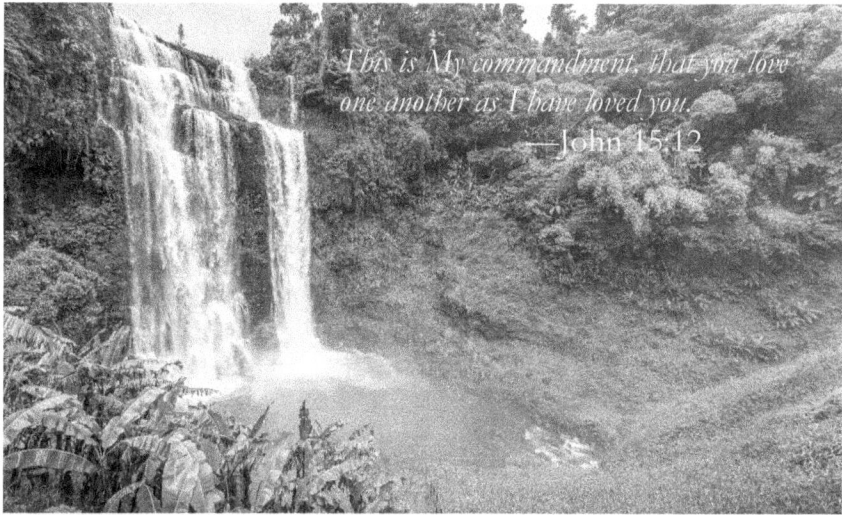
This is My commandment, that you love one another as I have loved you.
—John 15:12

More Than An Ice Cream Cone

Do you ever want to go somewhere just because of the people you will find there and the difference they make in your life? Sometimes we will go somewhere because we love someone and we know they love us. Sometimes it's because they are just happy people and fun to be around, bringing a touch of joy to the day. Sometimes it is because they are kind, or honest, or helpful, or caring or because they make us feel like we matter.

I also know people who refuse to go somewhere if certain other people will be present; even if their absence brings a void to the circle of people attending who love them. So not only do they miss out, but others suffer because of their inability to accept love and get along.

Sometimes people won't show up because they just don't like someone that will be there, or because they have an offense that hasn't been forgiven. Whatever their reason, they are missing out. They aren't free. They are actually being controlled by the person they are at odds with.

God is a God of love and wants us to love one another. If His Spirit lives in us, we have God in our life. If God is love (and He is) and if God's love is made complete in us (it will, if we let it), that love should be flowing through us to those around us.

No one has seen God at any time. If we love one another, God abides in us, and His love has been perfected in us.—1 John 4:12.

If we are willing to show each other the mercy and grace that God shows us, our life will be happier—and our health won't suffer. The Lord warns in 1 John 4:20-21: *If someone says, "I love God," and hates his brother, he is a liar; for he who does not love his brother whom he has seen, how can he love God whom he has not seen? And this commandment we have from Him: that he who loves God must love his brother also.*

The way we treat others may be their only evidence of God. That's a very sobering thought. We may have no idea what a person lives with or has endured in their life. But that shouldn't matter. We should reflect Christ's love to everyone, no matter where they have come from or what their past is. Romans 3:23, *for all have sinned and fall short of the glory of God,* and in Leviticus 19:33-34 NIV, *When a foreigner resides among you in your land, do not mistreat them. The foreigner residing among you must be treated as your native-born. Love them as yourself, ... I am the LORD your God.*

It's interesting to note, God rebukes those who only embrace the rich or popular. Romans 2:11 ESV says, *For God shows no partiality.* And in James 2:1-4 NIV, *My brother and sisters, believers in our glorious Lord Jesus Christ must not show favoritism. Suppose a man comes into your meeting wearing a gold ring and fine clothes, and a poor man in filthy old clothes also comes in. If you show special attention to the man wearing fine clothes and say, "Here's a good seat for you," but say to the poor man, "You stand there" or "Sit on the floor by my feet," have you not discriminated among yourselves and become judges with evil thoughts?*

There are a number of places I could list here, besides our church families, where I really enjoy going, but I want to focus on one particular place. God gave us this family! He just introduced us to them and then planted them down deep into our hearts. Let me introduce to you Todd and Michelle.

We first met Todd when we stopped at the ice cream stand near where we had recently moved. It was a hot, balmy day and we decided that after the exertion of moving, we needed a treat. Fortunately no one else was in line so we could take our time looking through all the delicious choices and one by one dismiss one flavor in favor of another out of the 22 to choose from.

Todd and Michelle own the ice cream stand. They are an adorable middle-aged couple with two precious teens. Todd is up every morning at 6:00am to start the day picking up trash behind the bear that vandalizes them every night after they close. (Did I tell you we moved to the mountains?) Then they are wiping down, sterilizing, and preparing food for the day, because—they don't just sell ice cream. They have lunch choices too. They usually open early and close at 8pm.

No matter whom you are or what time of the day it is, you are greeted with a smile and dancing eyes by both of them. Once you tell Michelle what you want, her response is always, "You got it." They both laugh easily but are just as willing to talk seriously and share their hearts.

When we first met Todd, Michelle wasn't there. He was on his own for the moment. We were about to leave when the Lord put on my heart to ask him what we could remember in prayer for him. He was surprised, but had a request. We prayed and God gave me more to pray over him.

The next time we came, Michelle was at the window and Todd was working the back. When he saw us he said to Michelle, "These are the people I told you about—the lady who prayed for me."

"Oh," Michelle exclaimed. "Todd told me about you."

With Love Overflowing

In a few minutes we were chatting and giggling as though we had known each other for years. Michelle giggles easily.

Prayer opened the door to friendship. We love them and it is easy to see that they care for people. They are generous, witty, and always have a kind word for everyone. In fact, it seems to me that everyone in line becomes their friends. We really love them!

We thought we were going in for an ice cream cone, but we ended up with more family! Sometimes we don't come in for anything but to check on them and see how they're doing. We just enjoy seeing them and chatting for a few minutes if they're not busy.

They make a difference—not just their ice cream! We go for more than an ice cream cone because they are magnetic! Thank you Todd and Michelle for your open hearts ... for sharing your genuine caring.

They made me wonder, what do I do or how do I act? Do I attract people? Am I as open and accepting as they model? Do others see Jesus in me? I want to reflect God's love and acceptance and invite people to feel welcome by how I act. I want my life to be magnetic, too.

Love Overflowed:

Thank You Father for this dear family You have given us. Please continue to bless them and use them to bring joy to those they serve. Please give us Your love—a true love for anyone You bring into our lives—even if we were to find them difficult.

How about you? Whom do you attract? What kind of effect do you have on people? Do you look for opportunities to make a difference for good? Are you ready to love with Jesus' love? Does your life offer "more than an ice cream cone?"

The nursing child shall play by the cobra's hole, And the weaned child shall put his hand in the viper's den. They shall not hurt nor destroy in all My holy mountain ...—Isaiah 11:8-9

Nest Of Rattlesnakes

It was early but was already hot on a beautiful summer morning. The boys had finished their breakfast and were restless from the heat. The tree in front of the house had beautiful foliage which gave us a nice shady spot for picnics and relaxation.

Matthew, about three and a half and Geoffrey, just over two years old had already parked their Tonka trucks under the tree. It was a pleasant place for them to play. I could keep my eyes on them while I finished cleaning the kitchen.

I asked them if they would like to go out and play for a while. Both were enthusiastic. They already had some ideas of what they wanted to do once outside. They grabbed their little shovels and buckets and headed for the door. Big brother Matthew in the lead helped his little brother down the steps.

They had not been out there long when I looked out the window and could not see them. As I was checking the yard I heard Matthew call, "Mommy, come see long worms!"

"Long worms?! Where are you?"

"Here."

With Love Overflowing

I looked around, quickly trying to follow his voice. What were they doing under the front porch deck? It was cool there and all dirt, a good place to dig … but when I looked under there and saw my two small boys sitting in the middle of a rattlesnake nest filled with baby snakes. I panicked. If I tried to reach in and grab them out I could stir up the snakes and the boys could have been covered with bites. I told them to sit still and I would be back to help them with the "worms." I ran for a rake and shovel. Jesus help me! Protect my sons!

As I was running back with my weapons, our neighbor, an older man, came by in his pickup truck and waved, then stopped to talk. I just kept running screaming, "the boys are in a rattlesnake nest!"

He jumped out of his truck, grabbed his shovel from the back, and followed me at a run. "Let me do this," he yelled

He wasn't as shaken as I was, and had much more experience than I. He reached under the deck and threw his shovel over the baby rattlesnakes and dragged them out from under the deck so he could deal with them.

While he was busy with the nest of snakes, I was busy getting my sons out from under the deck, checking them over, asking questions, holding them close and thanking God for his watchful care and protection.

Rattlesnakes come into our lives in many different ways and forms. In Genesis 3:1 ESV, the first book of the Bible, we are told, *Now the serpent was more crafty than any other beast of the field that the LORD God had made. He said to the woman, "Did God actually say, 'You shall not eat of any tree in the garden'?"* The enemy, Satan, tries to sneak up on us. Maybe he tempts you in your appetite, in your willingness to lie, deceive, gossip or complain.

A rattlesnake in your life could be an attitude or addiction of any kind. It will eventually "bite" you and inject poison that can dangerously threaten your life—eternal life. I could list a number of sins "evils" but if a rattlesnake has hold of you, you know it. It is time to deal with it. Get out the shovel and whack him on the head.

We have nothing to fear. Our God sends help when we call out to Him. We need to be alert, because according to 1 Peter 5:8-9, *Be sober, be vigilant; because your adversary the devil walks about like a roaring lion, seeking whom he may devour. Resist him, steadfast in the faith, knowing that the same sufferings are experienced by your brotherhood in the world.*

You're not alone in this. None of us have wings or a halo yet. We are in the struggle of life together learning to be overcomers—growing. We can be encouraged that when we are following Jesus he assures us in Luke 10:19, *Behold, I give you the authority to trample on serpents and scorpions, and over all the power of the enemy, and nothing shall by any means hurt you.*

Even though I walk through the valley of the shadow of death, I will fear no evil, for you are with me; your rod and your staff, they comfort me. You prepare a table before me in the presence of my enemies; you anoint my head with oil; my cup overflows.—Psalm 23:4-5 ESV.

With Love Overflowing

Love Overflowed:

Things could have been so different!!! Thank you Jesus for Your Divine protection of the innocent and unwary in the middle of a nest of rattlesnakes. Even when we don't realize we are in danger and aren't aware of Your presence, You lovingly watch over us and intervene.

they will pick up serpents, and if they drink any deadly poison, *it will not hurt them; ...*—Mark 16:18 NASB.

For He shall give His angels charge over you, to keep you in all your ways. You shall tread upon the lion and the cobra, The young lion and the serpent you shall trample underfoot.—Psalm 91:11, 13.

What rattlesnakes are you dealing with, ignoring—or hiding from? Stop hiding or procrastinating. God promises in James 1:21 ASV, *Wherefore putting away all filthiness and overflowing of wickedness, receive with meekness the implanted word, which is able to save your souls.*

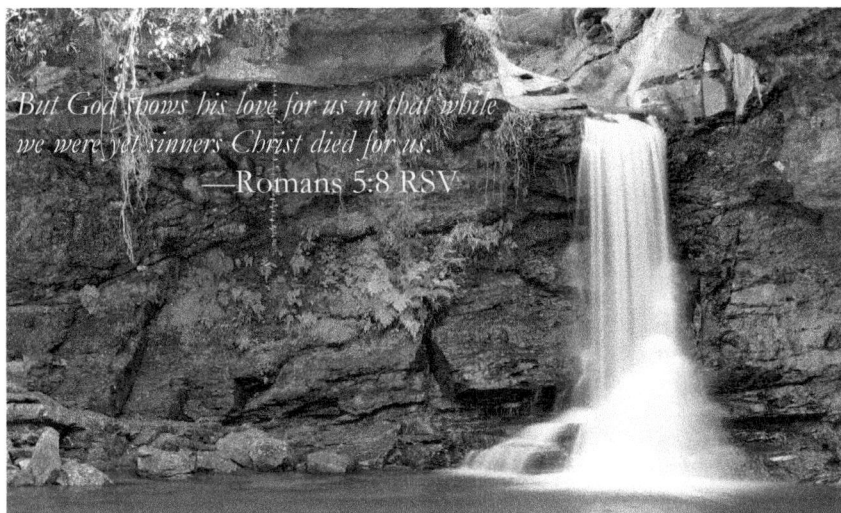
But God shows his love for us in that while we were yet sinners Christ died for us.
—Romans 5:8 RSV

No Manners Night

Our sons grew up in a very legalistic home. There were many "rules" that they were expected to abide by—some realistic, some a bit overdone.

One thing that was expected was good manners; particularly at mealtime. They were told to dress just so, to not put their elbows on the table, to use the right utensil, not to chew with their mouths open, etc. etc. Now I can't object to those rules. I was just uncomfortable that they had to be on their best behavior so much of the time. It seemed to me that since they were young children, mealtime should be a bit more enjoyable, not overwrought with instruction and correction. Let's take pleasure in each others' company and give our food a chance to digest!

Beginning to sense the tension mounting in the guys, I decided it might be nice if we would give the boys a break. I checked in with their dad about it and he agreed with my plan, saying just do it while I'm away.

So one night when Dad was away on a trip, I announced just before dinnertime that tonight would be "no manners night." They asked what that meant. I said, "Tonight if you want to put your elbows on the table or relax a bit, you may."

I was not ready for what hit! Little did I know how very pent up the boys were. We often had our larger meal midday and a lighter meal for our last meal of the day. I decided that maybe something like applesauce on peanut butter toast would be a 'safe' meal.

Was I ever wrong. The boys went wild! When the first spoonful of applesauce shot across the room, I was bewildered.

The heart is deceitful above all things, and desperately corrupt; who can understand it?—Jeremiah 17:9 RSV.

I wasn't going to go back on my word so I said, "Just remember that whatever mess you create, you also have to clean up. There are consequences for your actions."

Don't be misled—you cannot mock the justice of God. You will always harvest what you plant.—Galatians 6:7 NLT.

Long story short—they felt the cleanup would be worth it! The party got pretty wild. Truth is, I ate quickly and fled the table. The boys laughed and giggled in glee. They thought the cleanup was worth it. Actually they were true to their word and did a pretty good job cleaning up. I say pretty good job because even though I came to their rescue and offered a hand, we found applesauce later in places none of us thought to look—like the bottom of the kitchen cupboards!

A spiritual lesson came to mind from this: Sometimes we feel rebellious, life isn't what we expect and it seems to be spinning out of control. We rebel and make wrong decisions ... and there are consequences. We have to "clean up" behind ourselves.

Jesus in His love comes to our rescue. He is by our side helping us through the mess we have created. No matter what

126

we are struggling with spiritually, He is there to help us sort it out and is eager for us to see the truth of the matter—He loves us, and if we will, as 1 John 1:9 NLT says, *But if we confess our sins to him, he is faithful and just to forgive us our sins and to cleanse us from all wickedness.*

Love Overflowed:

Jesus showed me that too much was being demanded from our sons and their little hearts were starting to resist. He reminded me they need a joyful environment to be nurtured in. Jesus' watchful, liberating love overflowed to me and to them. Thank You Lord that You care about the little children and want them to come unto You. Thank You that You are merciful and slow to anger.

Do not be wise in your own eyes; Fear the LORD and turn away from evil.—Proverbs 3:7 NASB.

What changes do you need to make in your life to make it more pleasant and less stressful, for those around you? Do you need to adjust your disposition? Your responses? Do you need a "no manners night" at your house?

Gracious and merciful is the LORD, *slow to become angry, and overflowing with gracious love.*—Psalm 145:8 ISV.

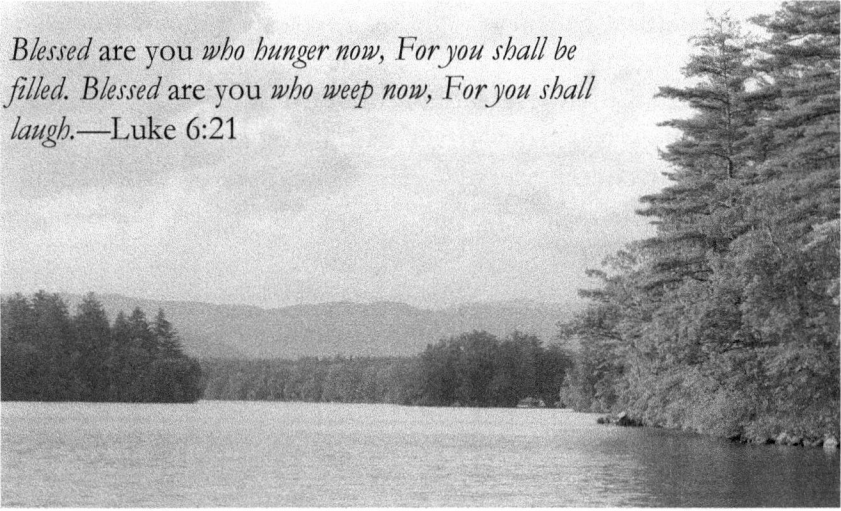

Only 35 Cents

It was the summer between my college semesters. I was looking forward to setting up my first apartment and working my new job at the hospital. Mom gave me a few supplies to get me started and I was settling in.

Somehow it hadn't occurred to me that I would not receive a paycheck at the end of my first week. The hospital was on a two-week pay schedule.

By the end of the first week, my scarce supply of food had diminished substantially. I hadn't lived there long enough to stock up. Three days into the following week I had empty cupboards and refrigerator. Four days until pay day. I began praying and scavenging. I emptied my old purses looking for change. I put my hands down the sides and back of the chairs and the sofa, hoping to find some loose coins. After my search, I held only 35 cents in my hand. There was nowhere else to look.

I thanked God for the money, asked His blessing over it and headed for the little neighborhood market a few blocks away. I wasn't sure what I was going to buy for that 35 cents so I took my time looking around, determining what I could get that would last four days. Then I saw a package of tortillas on sale for 25 cents. That gave me an idea. I picked up the tortillas and headed for the deli department. I smiled and said, "I don't know how much I can get with a dime, but I need ten cents worth of cheese please." He stood there and looked at me—a long while—then he said, "Sure." I got back a parcel with several slices of cheese.

I'm guessing there was some generosity bestowed upon me by that deli man! I divided my fare into four days and I made it until payday.

Jesus promises to take care of us—to provide for us—to watch over His children. As I was adjusting to life in the big world I learned the importance of budgeting and prioritizing as well as God's instruction to eat healthfully.

So whether you eat or drink or whatever you do, do it all for the glory of God.—1 Corinthians 10:31 NIV.

I also learned that unexpected emergencies could come up and drain your checkbook if you hadn't yet developed a savings account.

130

God had some interesting ways of keeping us afloat. I say "us" because after a few weeks, my old college roommate got a job at the hospital and moved in with me.

We were assessing our food supply one evening and were perplexed with our findings, when the phone rang. Someone had shared my name and number with this salesman. He was trying to set up a date for us to sponsor a Salad Master party at our apartment. I was about to say "No" when he told me he would be available the next evening if I could get people together by then. Then he ended with, "You don't have to worry about anything. I will be bringing dinner. I just hope someone wants to buy the cookware I'm selling." With payday a number of days off, my ears perked up. I let him know I was sure I could round up at least four people. He was fine with that on such short notice.

Love Overflowed:

Every time Carol and I faced a need our precious Jesus took care of it. Sometimes it was hard to comprehend how He could work things out so timely and stretch only 35 cents, yet with beneficient love He always came through.

They shall hunger no more, neither thirst any more; the sun shall not strike them, nor any scorching heat.—Revelation 7:16 RSV.

How can anyone resist a Savior overflowing with such love and care? When your cupboards are empty or your finances drained—Call upon Jesus. Matthew 6:33 NIV says, *But seek first his kingdom and his righteousness, and all these things will be given to you as well.* It's a matter of priorities. Put Jesus first, claim this Bible promise, and wait and watch. He loves to answer our prayers and see our excitement.

The promise in Matthew 6:33 is also for you. What provision are you in need of today?

With Love Overflowing

On Life's Busy Thoroughfares We Meet With Angels Unaware
—Helen Steiner Rice[†]

The unexpected kindness
    from an unexpected place,
A hand outstretched in friendship,
    a smile on someone's face,
A word of understanding
    spoken in an hour of trial
Are unexpected miracles
    that make life more worthwhile.
We know not how it happened
    that in an hour of need
Somebody out of nowhere
    proved to be a friend indeed.
For God has many messengers
    we fail to recognize,
But He sends them when we need them
    for His ways are wondrous wise!
So keep looking for an angel
    and keep listening to hear,
For on life's busy crowded streets
    you will find God's presence near.

[†]©1992 Helen Steiner Rice Foundation Fund, LLC, a wholly owned subsidiary of Cincinatti Museum Center

Jabez cried out to the God of Israel, "Oh, that you would bless me and enlarge my territory! Let your hand be with me, and keep me from harm so that I will be free from pain." And God granted his request.
—1 Chronicles 4:10 NIV

Passion To Share Jesus

When you love someone you can't help but talk about them. I love Jesus. I love to talk to Him and about Him. However, during my morning devotions I was feeling some disappointment. "It seems, Lord," I said, "that I haven't been doing much away from home for you lately. I think that it's time to expand my territory for you again." I opened my Bible to 1 Chronicles 4:10: *And Jabez called on the God of Israel saying, "Oh, that You would bless me indeed, and enlarge my territory, that Your hand would be with me, and that You would keep me from evil, that I may not cause pain!" So God granted him what he requested.* I once again claimed Jabez' prayer as my own. It had been a while since I had asked God to fill this request. Now, on this day, I was hopeful that my petition would again be answered.

Several years ago a friend had given me the little book *The Prayer of Jabez.* It was one of those 'friendships' where you felt a certain amount of obligation to do what needed to be done to nurture it along. Reluctantly I settled in one night to tackle this book that I was told I must read. I wanted to be able to say I had looked at it, but it quickly captured my attention. It had an incredible impact on my life. I began personal-

133

izing Jabez' petition that God would expand my territory for Him and within a short time I experienced amazing answers. I was thankful for this friend and his gift.

I lived in a small, somewhat isolated community in California. Within an hour of my prayer I received a call from New York asking permission to broadcast my sermons on their radio station.

Encouraged by the immediate answer to my prayer to broaden my territory for Jesus, I asked again. Two hours later, I received a call from Alaska asking me to be their guest speaker for a Women's Retreat. Two days later I received a call from a Christian television broadcasting station requesting some of my stories for a devotional book they were putting together for the new year.

Jesus is eager for the message of His love to go to all the world. Sometimes He waits for us to ask Him what He has in mind for us to do for His Kingdom's glory. Sometimes He extends an invitation. Sometimes He waits for us to ask Him.

You shall love the LORD your God with all your heart, with all your soul, and with all your strength. "And these words which I command you today shall be in your heart. You shall teach them diligently ...
—Deuteronomy 6:5-7.

We are all called to be ministers for Him. When we find ourselves put on the spot, to answer questions we feel unprepared to answer, if we have learned to depend upon the Holy Spirit, we will be able to speak with maturity beyond our years or experience, love beyond our own capabilities and have discernment beyond our knowledge. All this is ours because we have developed a concern for the eternal welfare of others, have submitted to Jesus and have placed our trust in the guidance and wisdom of the Holy Spirit.

When we give our heart to Jesus we are born anew in Christ. We become a new creation. 2 Corinthians 5:17 says,

Therefore, if anyone is in Christ, he is a new creation; old things have passed away; behold, all things have become new. Although we receive new life, that doesn't mean we have become perfect. We still have sinful habits that need to be refined and overcome. We need to adjust to this "new" way, but we will recognize our sinful tendencies because we have a new perspective—a new outlook on life. We will want to conform to Christ's image by how we treat others, how we live our life, the plans we make and the value we put on things. We will want to respond differently.

If you don't feel new, don't worry. Growth in Jesus takes time just as our physical growth takes time. The more time you invest in your relationship with Him, the more you will love Him and aspire to be like Him.

We were each designed for a purpose no one else can fill—an irreplaceable niche in God's work—to share our own passion for Jesus.

Thank You Lord for offering us "new life" to be a new creation for You. Please change our hearts and minds to conform to Your heart and mind, willing and in earnest to do Your will.

Love Overflowed:

This verse is powerful. It taught me that God means what He says. I claimed His promise and He enlarged my territory for His glory. Wherever I go today, whatever I am doing, whomever I speak to—I want to make a difference for good for Jesus because over and over I have experienced His love, and I want others to experience it too.

As Mordecai said to Queen Esther in Esther 4:14 NIV, *... And who knows but that you have come ... for such a time as this?*

With Love Overflowing

> Sometimes God redeems your story by surrounding you with people who need to hear your past, so it doesn't become their future.
> —Jon Acuff

This is your time—use it with boldness, with faith and love. What are you eager to do for our Lord? Do you have a passion to share Jesus?

Now may the God of hope fill you with all joy and peace as you believe in Him so that you may **overflow** *with hope by the power of the Holy Spirit.*—Romans 15:13 HCSB.

*God is our refuge and strength, A very present help in trouble. Therefore we will not fear, ...—*Psalm 46:1-2

Pushing A BMW

It had been a very busy morning. Usually I didn't leave the office during my lunch hour but that day I had an important errand to run during my break.

I was just getting on the freeway headed back to the office after running my errands when I saw a car with a young woman stuck right in the traffic lane. She had tried to climb up where it was safe, but there was no safe place for her.

Instead of continuing to merge, I stopped my car near her BMW and yelled, "You are not safe here."

I don't remember what happened next. I just know that her car was in a place where cars coming around the corner could crash into it and no one was safe with it there. Besides her life being at risk, there was the potential of a real pileup and many being hurt. The only quick solution was to get her car into the triangle area where the lane reduces and merges. I parked off the side of the road and ran across the highway, got behind her car and pushed. At least it would be out of the lane.

I can't imagine what I was thinking, but I cried out to God for help and with holy boldness I started pushing the

With Love Overflowing

BMW. There is no question that the angels pushed with me. The car was quickly moved out of the way. We were safe.

"Well that was something!" she said. We both looked at each other in astonishment and broke into laughter.

She had already called for a tow truck and was waiting for it to arrive. I handed her a blanket from my car, suggested she sit up on the bank in a safe place, and I headed back to work.

I learned the rest of the story from the following article printed in *The Union*—the town's newspaper, September 16, 1999:

Caption:

Woman in need was pleased to receive so much help

Article:

Okay, I admit it … I was pushing my luck. I thought I had enough gas to get to Nevada City, but as soon as I cleared the construction area on Highway 49 south of the 174 turn-off, my car came to a limp halt. While I managed to maneuver onto the shoulder, I was clearly in a precarious spot.

After calling AAA, I sat back to wait. Within seconds a woman stopped to help. Her name is Chaplain Derry, and she's from Sierra Nevada Memorial Hospital. She was concerned that I was parked in a dangerous location, and offered to push me … by hand. Now, I may have gotten a "C" in college physics, but I'm pretty sure that one small woman cannot move one, albeit small, BMW. But after saying a brief prayer, Chaplain Derry did precisely that—pushing my car to a safer spot. She even gave me a blanket to sit on while I waited.

By now, I was feeling particularly blessed. But there was more to come. Within seconds, a gentleman driving a white Dodge van pulled over. I explained the situation, and told him what Chaplain Derry had done. He handed me a bottle of icy water and said, "We're looking out for you." He was gone before I thought to ask his name.

Only minutes had gone by when the tow truck arrived. Then another one. I couldn't believe my good fortune … until one of the drivers told me that even with a few gallons of gas, it was unlikely that my car would start. Seems I have a little feature called fuel injection.

So I held my breath while he poured in the gas, got behind the wheel, turned the key … and the engine started. "That's not supposed to happen," he said. But I have a feeling Chaplain Derry knew it would.

With Love Overflowing

> To Chaplain Derry ... to the man in the white
> Dodge van ... and to the two tow-truck drivers
> from Dunivin's ... thanks for being there when
> I needed you. Most of all, thanks for renewing
> my faith in humanity ... and beyond.
>
> —Lynda Mansfield, Nevada City.

Lynda delivered my blanket back to the Chaplain's office at the hospital. A happy ending to an unexpected adventure!

Think about it. There are many things in life that we are incapable of doing alone, but if we cry out to God to help us, He is right there!

Love Overflowed:

Ohhh what love! He used me to protect and help another one of His daughters. Father, Your love overflows and You are irresistible, Jesus! How did I think I could push a BMW? That was only from You!

He gives power to the weak, And to those who have *no might He increases strength.*—Isaiah 40:29.

Do you need supernatural strength to accomplish something amazing? God is excited when you want to do great things for Him ... and for His children.

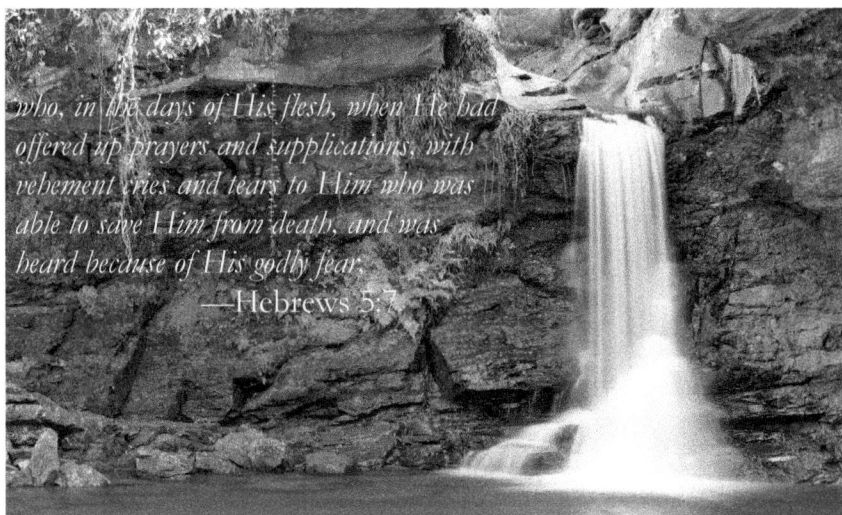

who, in the days of His flesh, when He had offered up prayers and supplications, with vehement cries and tears to Him who was able to save Him from death, and was heard because of His godly fear;
—Hebrews 5:7

Saving Mother's Life

We had recently accepted a new position as caretakers for a traveling singing group, The Heritage Singers. They had a lodge on a beautiful piece of property way up in the mountains, off the beaten trail. When the singers took a respite from their travels, they came there. The group was roughly 30 in number. I did the cooking and baking for them. My husband tended the garden and the grounds.

We lived in a small, very rustic two-bedroom log cabin on the grounds. We were detached from any outside communication. Cell phones had not yet come into existence.

It had been a long, busy day. I was exhausted. I couldn't wait to go to bed. No sooner had my head hit the pillow, I was out cold; but not for long ....

Around 2:15am I awoke with a start—an urgency. God spoke in the depths of my spirit, "Pray for your mother." I was still groggy, but I began to pray, not knowing what I was praying for. I began to doze. Again, God woke me up. "Pray for your mother." This time I sat up in bed and asked God to give me the words to pray for her. I didn't know why my mother needed prayer, but I prayed.

141

With Love Overflowing

Within minutes, even though I was cold, I slipped out of my blankets and fell to my knees pleading for her life. In Psalm 142:1 David says, *I cry out to the LORD with my voice; With my voice to the LORD I make my supplication.* I was doing just that. My heart was in distress over her and I began crying out to God. I prayed for over an hour—until I felt I had been released, then I climbed back into bed and slept.

The next day I headed to town some 40 minutes from the cabin to phone Mom. No answer. I waited around in case she was out feeding the horses. But where was Dad? I waited for over 30 minutes—no answer.

It was three days later before I could get back to town. I called again. This time Mom answered right away. I started out casually; then finally asked, "Why did God wake me up at 2am Sunday morning to pray for you?" Mom was quiet.

"I just got back from the hospital, Dee. You know that we live over an hour away from the hospital or any emergency assistance. Evidently, I was having a heart attack. I was scared. I didn't think I was going to make it. We got to the hospital in time, though. God had you start praying about the time we were heading for the car. It sounds like you prayed us all the way there. Your prayers to God saved my life."

Love Overflowed:

Thank You Lord that even without the telephone You got word to me that my mom's life was being threatened and called upon me to intercede to save Mother's life and for giving us more time with her. Thank You for Your compassionate love in sparing Mom.

And God will wipe away every tear from their eyes; there shall be no more death, nor sorrow, nor crying. There shall be no more pain, for the former things have passed away.—Revelation 21:4.

When God puts someone on your heart, do you stop and pray for them? You may not know what they are going through, but God is trusting you to intercede.

142

And we know that all things work together for good to those who love God, to those who are the called according to His purpose.—Romans 8:28

SpaghettiOs

I was busy making supper one evening when a disturbing phone call interrupted my meal preparation. The voice on the other end of the line stated, "I want to place my sons in your boarding school."

"I don't have a boarding school." I responded. "I homeschool my sons."

"Yes, you do have a boarding school. You are on this list that I found and I want my sons to go to your school."

I was about to contradict but the Lord said distinctly, "Listen!"

She continued, "May I come over this afternoon and take a look at your place?"

The Lord made it clear that I was to allow her to come so I agreed. When I got off the phone I began complaining to the Lord. "What's going on, Father? I'm worn out. I'm down to two sons left at home and I need a break from having other kids in for a while. I just want my two."

God said, "Listen."

With Love Overflowing

I was quiet. He didn't say anything so I spoke again. "Alright, if You want these kids to come here, then when they arrive, I need to feel love for them as my own the minute they come in the door."

They came. I did! I immediately felt love for them as though I had always known them—as though they were my own. There were three boys. The oldest was 11, the next nine, and the youngest four. My husband and I listened as their mother shared her story. Their father was in jail and she needed to work full-time. She needed a place for her two oldest sons.

I knew in my heart what had to be done. I looked at my husband and he looked at me knowingly. I said, "We will take them on one condition—it's all three or none."

She was excited to hear that. We made a deal and she said she would come back the following week with their things.

Their things consisted of one suitcase with clothes for all three and each had a new sleeping bag and pillow. They were so excited. They had never had their own sleeping bag. They couldn't wait to try it out ... only I now had complicated things for them unintentionally. I had a bedroom ready for them. It had a bunk bed and a single bed all with sheets and bedspreads, dressers, bookcase, lamps, and a closet. I didn't know the boys had never had a bed to sleep in. They were accustomed to sleeping on the floor with a sheet or blanket. They couldn't believe they had their own beds!

We struck a compromise during their settling-in time. They could sleep on the beds in their sleeping bags.

In a short time, stories of their past began to unfold. All three boys were timid, insecure and easily frightened. They had lived by robbing garbage cans at night for food—to the point of hiding bones under their pillow so they would have something to suck on if they couldn't find food the next day. Their mother, who we found was addicted to drugs, would

144

often leave them alone for days on end. They didn't know when to expect her or if she would return. They roamed the neighborhood and looked after each other—the eldest assuming responsibility for his younger brothers.

Their "remembering" brought tears to my heart as well as my eyes. I didn't want to quiet them when they began sharing. It was important that they were able to talk it out, but it was often painfully difficult to listen to them and imagine the terror that erupted in their hearts when exposed to unexpected situations in their young lives.

When I tucked them in bed at night I would assure them of my love for them and say, "I'm sending you to bed with kisses and hugs." I continued to find ways to substantiate my love. When we were in class doing our spelling or writing, I would laugh and remind them that X meant kisses and O meant hugs. Sometimes on their graded papers I would write XO.

One evening my husband and I were going out for a few hours. We told all the boys, our new ones and our sons, who the babysitter was who would be there with them. Our new boys became very frightened. "Are you coming back? How long will you be gone? Can we wait up for you?

What do we do if you don't come back? Where should we go?"

I went to my room and cried and asked God what to do. The Lord put something wonderful on my heart to do for them. I went to the market and picked up some SpaghettiOs. Not just any SpaghettiOs, but the ones that had X's and O's. I wish they still made them.

I told the boys they could have some for dinner and would leave a can on the counter to come look at as a reminder that we loved them; we were sending them hugs and kisses and would be back later that night. God knew it would reassure them. It worked. They even went to bed and went to sleep.

With Love Overflowing

Even though we had made a deal about "tuition," Mom didn't come through. In fact, once the boys and their possessions were delivered to us we didn't hear from her and were unable to contact her.

Remember, it is sin to know what you ought to do and then not do it.
        —James 4:17 NLT.

We did however hear from the boys' father. He would call from jail. We would talk to him about Jesus and His love and forgiveness, trying to encourage him and offer him hope for his future. Occasionally his mother would also call from Louisiana and talk to the boys.

Dear brothers and sisters, if another believer is overcome by some sin, you who are godly should gently and humbly help that person back onto the right path ...—Galatians 6:1 NLT.

We had had them for almost six months now. We wanted to take them on vacation with us; but that meant travel on the airlines and we had no legal papers that would allow us to have them with us.

My husband and I planned a day to try to track their mother down. After a lot of praying and following leads—we caught up with her. She was high. We asked her to sign custody papers so we could take the children on vacation. We explained and she agreed. The papers were signed and in hand! It would be almost six months before we would hear from her again.

Several months after we got custody we decided we wanted to adopt the boys. We thought we'd better be careful how we broached the subject with her when we had contact with her again.

We had been trying to locate her so we could initiate adoption when we discovered there was a warrant out for her

146

arrest for fraud and forgery. We knew it would be pretty difficult to track her now … But surprise of surprises ….

We received a call from her attorney demanding that
we release the children to their mother. I was stunned. I let the
attorney know that the children were safe and happy and exactly where their mother had left them but that we had heard
nothing from her in months. She had abandoned them and we
had been trying to locate her. I shared that we had just discovered there was a warrant out for her arrest and it might not be
in the children's best interest to have them go with her at this
time.

The attorney stated firmly that their mother would be
there that night to pick them up and that I was to have their
things ready. If not, the police would be on our doorstep to
get the boys. (We later found out that her mother was visiting
from another country and demanded that she have her grand-
children there when she arrived.)

We knew this wasn't a good situation so we called their
paternal grandmother who was a licensed chiropractor with an
excellent reputation. She lived in another state but was our
only hope for the boys to get to a safe place.

Everything happened so fast. We had no immediate re-
course. The boys were both excited to see their mother and
torn because they didn't want to leave us. I was shattered.

They left that night and I fell on my knees before the
Lord, brokenhearted and grieving … grieving as though they
had died. God had given me a love for them as my own and I
felt as though life was being pulled from me with their depar-
ture. As I sobbed before God, suddenly a thought came to my
mind so I prayed it. "Father, I had asked You to give me a
love for these boys as my own if You wanted them to come
here—and You did. Now I pray that since You have removed
them, You will remove that love and stop this pain in my heart
and my grief." Again God honored my prayer.

With Love Overflowing

As I sit here writing this story, I am again reminded that when God calls us to do something, He enables. He gives us what we need to help us accomplish what He has called us to do. These children needed love and a safe place. He brought them to us.

Love Overflowed:

God sent children and filled my heart with His abundant love for them. They blessed our home for almost a year and then in God's redemptive love and knowledge of my future, He gave their grandmother custody of them. They were able to grow up in a safe place where they would be secure and loved, able to have their own home and complete their education with family.

Thank You Jesus that all things work together for good.

Is not this the fast that I choose: to loose the bonds of wickedness, to undo the straps of the yoke, to let the oppressed go free, and to break every yoke? Is it not to share your bread with the hungry and bring the homeless poor into your house; when you see the naked, to cover him, and not to hide yourself from your own flesh?—Isaiah 58:6-7 ESV.

Does someone need to experience the security of your love? Do you need to open your heart and your home? Do you need a can of X & O SpaghettiOs?

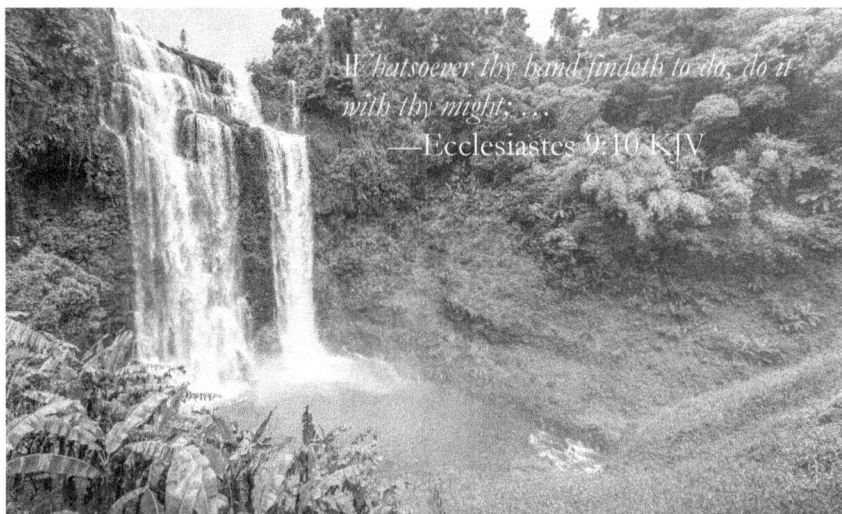

Whatsoever thy hand findeth to do, do it with thy might; ....
—Ecclesiastes 9:10 KJV

Tackling The Difficult

I was in the kitchen preparing dinner when the front door opened and my son called, "You'd better come quick and see Nathan."

With that tone of voice and a request like that, I didn't wait. I immediately stopped what I was doing and came.

"Where is he?" I asked.

"Find him." I was challenged.

Hmmm. What was going on? I searched Daniel's face for a clue. He glanced up so I searched "up." I couldn't see anything. Then I heard, "Hi Mom." from a distance away. Where was he?

"Hi Mom."

I looked towards the sound of his voice and I looked up. Oh help!!! I could see my son waving at me from the top of an old grandfather cedar tree. He must have been between 40-50 feet up. My stomach was in knots. Thank God he was safe, but now he needed to get down. It's one thing to climb up, but champion tree climbers will tell you that the more

With Love Overflowing

dangerous part of the climb is going down! Please protect him, Lord Jesus!

I learned several things from Nathan that day worth applying to my life. First, he was brave enough to tackle something difficult, no matter how overwhelming it appeared. Am I willing to brave a challenge when it appears overwhelming to me? Are you?

But I realized something else. There is great joy in sharing our victories with each other—especially someone we know loves us. Joy shared multiples the reward of our victory.

I wonder how many things I have stepped away from pursuing because I wasn't brave enough to move forward. Satan, the great deceiver wants us to feel inadequate—in anything we attempt. God on the other hand, wants to empower us for success.

Love Overflowed:

Thank You Jesus for giving my son such courage and for keeping him safe. Thank You for the lessons his victory spoke to me.

God, Whose heart is filled with love for us, assures us in Psalm 32:8, *I will instruct you and teach you in the way you should go; I will guide you with My eye.* Therefore we have nothing to fear. He is the God of successes. His love empowers.

What will you brave today? What will your next victory be? Are you up to tackling the difficult? You can! With God by your side, anything is possible.

150

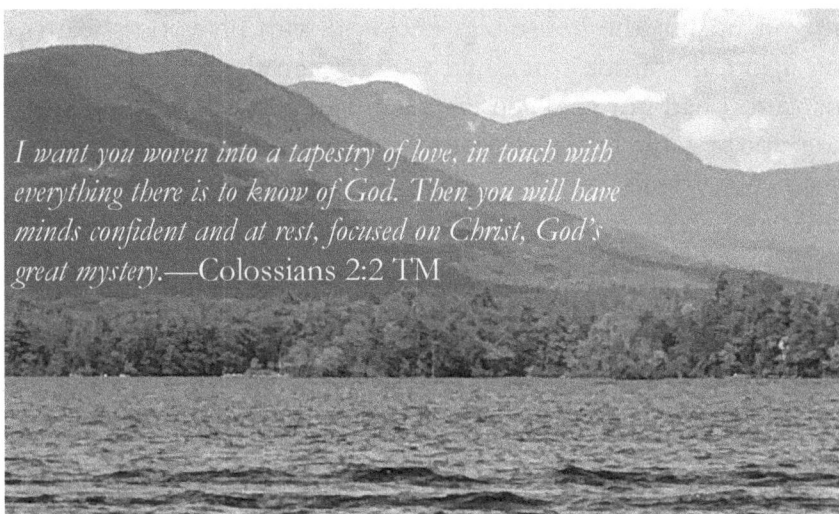

I want you woven into a tapestry of love, in touch with everything there is to know of God. Then you will have minds confident and at rest, focused on Christ, God's great mystery.—Colossians 2:2 TM

Tapestry

A visitor arrived at church. She was beautiful, early middle-aged, large blue eyes and bleached blonde hair. The look on her face revealed her discomfort and insecurity of being there. I happened to be walking through the foyer when she arrived. She was alone. Noting her timidity, I approached with an inviting welcome. She made our church her home church.

We soon became good friends and often got together during the week. Her husband was a dentist and seemed to have no interest in joining her for church. We would talk on the phone during the week and often laugh and carry on. This soon piqued his interest and he agreed to attend church functions with her, just not the church service.

After interacting with them as a couple a number of times at church socials, we invited them over for dinner. We were in the middle of a building project, but that didn't stop me from using my gift of hospitality. We enjoy people and enjoy sharing and serving.

We had just allowed the children to move their beds from the garage into the living-room area. The sheetrock was

With Love Overflowing

not yet up but the house was enclosed with plywood sheathing. From the inside you could see between the framing as the insulation had not yet been installed. I had just completed setting up the table in the soon-to-be dining room when they arrived. My friend had been over to the house a number of times and was aware of the conditions.

I soon realized that when you are building, your focus is on the job at hand—the accomplishment of the moment. Daily life is so busy you easily overlook the mundane chores—like dusting between studs—until company arrives and its glaring presence is telling. That is what happened to me when this dear couple arrived.

There was a foundation block outside the front door that provided a step to enter the house. When you came in, a short wall of unfinished framing caught your eye. They entered and Dave was ashen. All over his face you could see written "Where am I and what am I doing here?" Of course I had assumed that my friend, his wife, would have told him about the conditions. Obviously not.

As I followed his gaze I was horrified to see a huge spider web draped between the boards. I turned around and looked at him and said, "Have you never been anywhere before where they weave their own tapestry?" He burst out laughing. The evening ended up a success despite my being oblivious to the critters that had moved in.

As I was reflecting on this story, some "tapestry" quotations came to mind:

> A wonderful realization will be the day you realize that you are unique in all the world. The world is an incredible unfulfilled tapestry, and only you can fulfill that tiny space that is yours.
>
> —Leo Buscaglia

We can be assured that God has a place for each of us—a place only we individually can fill. He called us forth for such a time as this. He wrote in John 15:11 AMP, *I have told you these things so that My joy* and *delight may be in you, and that your joy may be made full* and *complete* and *overflowing.*

Our grandson Anthony loves to play hide and seek. When he covers his eyes he thinks *we* can't see *him*. Many, like Anthony, seem to think that if they turn their eyes away and don't acknowledge your presence, that they too are not seen. There is sadly, so much fear and insecurity in this world. We don't engage people, instead we hide. Jesus has a plan for each of us and we are all unique and important to Him. If we don't fulfill our "tiny space" the tapestry will be incomplete.

Pain and suffering are the dark strands through the tapestry of your life, providing the shadows that give depth and dimension to the masterpiece God is fashioning within you.
—Joseph Girzone

Life for many is like a glass that drops from our hands hitting the kitchen floor hard, shattering slivers of glass everywhere. Life problems we create or are imposed on us are like those shattered pieces. They are hard to clean up. We think it's clean but there are slivers we don't catch until we feel the pain in our bare foot. We call out to God and He comes behind us "digging out" those slivers so we can heal and cleaning up our messes. He can turn our brokenness into something beautiful—something special.

GOD, pick up the pieces. Put me back together again. You are my praise!—Jeremiah 17:14 MSG.

How we deal with life's challenges, pain and suffering will affect the tapestry we are creating of our life. God wants to fashion us into something beautiful if we will let Him work with us, in us and through us.

> But things are not always what they seem for when you turn the tapestry over you can see the astonishing beauty of what God is doing in your life. The truth is that we don't see what God sees, but He occasionally gives us a glimpse at what He is weaving into the fabric of our lives.
>
> —Tim Young,
> Author of *Heartstone*

One of those beautiful moments of what God is doing in our lives was when we stopped at Denny's on the way down to Florida. At the end of our meal, I asked the waitress if there was anything we could remember in prayer to thank her for her good service—besides her tip. She responded with tears in her eyes and had several requests of considerable importance. After our prayer, she was quite emotional. She excused herself and we started getting our things together to leave. Before we could get out of our chairs, she was back and asked if she could bring a co-worker out for us to pray for. So we did. Then as we left, the cashier said that she saw we had been praying for others and asked if we could pray for her also.

What fun we had. God turned Denny's into a "house of prayer" because we had turned our lives over to Him to do something beautiful with them. We were willing to share our love with others and our love for Him.

God gives us so many opportunities if we will boldly "seize the moment." And He loves us so much He is more than willing to help us pick up the shattered pieces of our lives when we call upon His name. We might cover our face and try to hide, but our Lord knows our name and He knows where we are. If we are willing, He will use us to bless others and in so doing we will realize how important we are to Him.

Let God put the shattered pieces of your life back together and make something beautiful of your future so that when He is finished, you too will be a beautiful tapestry.

Love Overflowed:

God shows up in unexpected ways. With the help of a little spider and a comical remark about "weaving your own tapestry," our loving God of relationships set us up for a growing friendship.

Zephaniah 3:17 says, ... *He will quiet* you *with His love* ...

Thank you Father for quieting my heart in the midst of embarrassment. Thank You that in the midst of discouragement You help us remember all the times You have provided a way. Make us keenly aware of the blessings all around us and help us to be continually grateful for the confirmation of Your love in all of life.

We all have black thread in our tapestry, which shows off the colored threads. Have you used humor to lighten up a difficult moment? Are you grateful for the dark times that made the colorful happy times even better? Will you let Jesus complete the tapestry He has started in *you?*

If you truly love God, you will love your neighbor. It does not make any difference if he loves you or not.

—Fr. Thomas Augustine Judge, C.M.

All scripture is inspired by God and profitable for teaching, for reproof, for correction, and for training in righteousness, that the man of God may be complete, equipped for every good work.

—2 Timothy 3:16-17 RSV

Those Who Have Gone Before

It had been a long trip. We were on our third day of travel. My husband is a good driver but driving from Florida to New Hampshire is both pleasant and grueling depending on the traffic and the weather.

It was late. We debated whether to stay in Scranton, PA or continue on home. We had another five hours at least. Men like to push it. My husband wanted to keep going even if it meant arriving in the middle of the night. I didn't see the wisdom in that.

As I was contemplating the effect of our choice it occurred to me that my husband had mentioned several times that he had not been to his brother's or mother's gravesite in the Bronx, NY for many years. He shared he would really like to go soon. Knowing the importance of honoring those who have gone before us and acknowledging their life and contribution to life, I suggested that if we stayed in Scranton we could get up early in the morning and stop at the cemetery. He liked that idea, but informed me he did not know where the graves were.

With Love Overflowing

God's love is interesting and amazing to me. He knows even the small things that are meaningful and important to us and even without us asking, He orchestrates circumstances for us to fulfill those desires. I call those "Kisses from Heaven."

The next day we headed for the area where my husband thought the cemetery was. There was one section after another. He had no idea where to begin but God lead us step by step. We finally found an office. We gave the volunteer the names of who we were looking for. After some searching she came back with the information needed to locate their gravesites.

Little did we know when we decided to stay over, that Saturday morning from 9-12 was the only time the office was open. Had we come any other time or any other day, there would have been no one available to guide us.

Memories are important, so are the lessons we learn from those who have gone before us. The people we spend time with contribute and can shape who we are. The Lord wants us to remember them, but He wants us to move on, too. In Jeremiah 31:13 NLT He assures us, ... *I will turn their mourning into joy. I will comfort them and exchange their sorrow for rejoicing.*

The Bible is full of stories of men and women who have preceded us. Their memories remain with us through the written word. The lessons are there for examples of both right and wrong choices. There are lessons of extreme faith and lessons of those who walked in pride and disobedience, but everything written is for us, including the promises made to those who lived in the past. The instruction to them is for us.

Love Overflowed:

God's word is true. It is sure. It offers hope for your future, and serves as a guide. As you apply His word to your life and choose to accept the gift of Jesus' sacrifice as penalty and payment for your sins; as you choose to love and obey

158

Him, to accept His forgiveness, you are assured an eternal home in heaven with God, His holy angels and those you love.

Study those who have gone before and learn from them. Come to Jesus and learn of Him. He is eagerly waiting. Remember what was done for you in the past and say "Yes Lord."

Have you said yes? It's time. I challenge you to make that a choice of your heart today. Take a step forward. Walk with Him. His love never fails.

For whatever was written in former days was written for our instruction, that by steadfastness and by the encouragement of the scriptures we might have hope.—Romans 15:4 RSV.

Therefore, as you have received Christ Jesus the Lord, so walk in Him, having been firmly rooted and now being built up in Him and established in your faith, just as you were instructed, and overflowing with gratitude.—Colossians 2:6-7 NASB.

Sing to the LORD a new song; sing to the LORD, all the earth. Sing to the LORD, praise his name; proclaim his salvation day after day. Declare his glory among the nations, his marvelous deeds among all peoples. For great is the LORD and most worthy of praise; he is to be feared above all gods.—Psalm 96:1-4 NIV

Three Pianos From My Father

When I was a little girl, probably about the age of 10 or 12, I took accordion lessons. I enjoyed the accordion, but my hearts desire was to learn to play the piano. We really didn't have room for a piano, so the accordion had to do. I took lessons for over seven years and performed in bands with other young accordionists and played in parades on floats.

In my sophomore year of high school I received sad news that my best friend was moving away. Her family was loading up the moving truck the same weekend my parents were going to be out of town for a special anniversary weekend. Consequently, I had no way of getting to her house to share our final goodbyes and give each other a parting hug.

Sunday afternoon I gave her a call and asked how all the packing was going. She reported that they were almost finished but they were perplexed because there was not enough room in the moving truck to load their piano.

"Piano," I exclaimed. "I've always wanted a piano. If you can't take it with you, and plan to leave it behind, is there any way your parents could get it to my house?"

"I don't know." she said. "I'll talk to them and call you back."

Excitedly I waited for a return call. Could it really be that my dream would come true today? Wouldn't my parents be surprised!

A few minutes later she called back. "My parents are actually hoping to sell it."

I was so close yet so far away from my dream being realized. My little head started working. I didn't have any money. My parents weren't here to "convince" of my desperate need. What could I do? Then my young head came up with a solution. I had always wanted to play the piano instead of the accordion. Why not trade my accordion for their piano?

I called her back and offered to trade. Her parents said that would work. So in a few short hours the trade was made. I handed over my beautiful shining accordion and against the back wall of our dining room rested a rather old, worn and battered-looking piano. But it was mine and I was thrilled.

I sat down to play my first piece, and sadly realized the piano was out of tune. I assumed it happened during the move. The next few hours as we waited for our parents' return, I sat at the piano practicing with determination so I could surprise mom when she walked in. That never happened.

It had not occurred to me that when you came in the front door you looked through the dining room and the first thing you saw was the piano. That's exactly what happened when Mom and Dad returned. Instead of hello, it was, "Where did that come from?"

Of course I was still excited and quickly explained the whole story. Mother was excited too, but not a happy excited. The tone of her voice elevated, "You mean you traded your beautiful expensive accordion for this piece of junk? Do you have any idea how much that accordion cost? Young lady, you have lost your accordion and this piano is mine."

162

Within a moment my joy was turned to sorrow. Nevertheless, there it was—a piano in my home that I had always dreamed of. It may have become mother's, but I still got to use it while I lived there. As far as I was concerned God had heard my prayer. Jeremiah 29:12, *Then you will call upon Me and go and pray to Me, and I will listen to you.*

God knew my heart. The reason I wanted a piano was to worship Him. I just wanted to sing and play the piano and worship my Lord. It was a dream that lingered within me. When I went off to college, I took piano lessons. But due to health reasons I was only there one semester. Years went by with the longing still in my heart.

Time passed. Married now and designing our first home to be built, we both decided to include a special place in the living room where a baby grand piano could be placed. The house was built, years went by; an old upright filled that area. Not a baby grand.

It wasn't until I was alone and had just completed my Doctor of Ministry degree and Chaplain's Board Certification that I got my baby grand.

Shortly after graduation I was headed to an appointment in a large city about an hour away. As I was driving on the highway the Lord directed me to look to the left. There I saw a large sign that said, PIANO CLEARANCE THIS WEEK. He then spoke to my heart and said, "I want you to stop there on the way back."

Having completed my appointment I was heading back home. I had no idea where I was supposed to get off the freeway in order to go to this piano sale. I didn't see a sign from this direction. God directed me to the exit before I passed the correct road. He helped me drive right to the sale.

There were pianos all over the parking lot, too numerous to count. Many of them were exquisite. There were only a few that had prices on them. As I wandered through the various pianos, I thought, 'I'll look for one the color of the wood

163

on the wainscoting in that area of the living room.' I came to a piano different from the others that I thought would be perfect. There was no price on it. But it was lovely.

I ran my hands along the keyboard, dreaming now. I touched the keys. What a beautiful tone. I said to myself, "I'm sure this is more than I have put away." I had started saving for my baby grand. I had $550 put away in that account. I was about to walk away to look for something I knew would be less expensive, when a young saleswoman came up to me. What do you think of this piano?" she asked.

"I think it's absolutely lovely," I mused.

"Would you like to have it?" she queried.

"I would love to have it!" I responded, "But it's obvious to me by its appearance that it's more than I can afford."

"Well how much can you afford?"

"I won't even tell you because I would hate to offend you. I have been wanting a piano forever and I have just begun saving for one again."

"How much do you have saved?" she asked.

"I have $550."

"Why don't you come with me and talk to the manager. Make him an offer. We have a number of ways we can help people actualize their dreams."

"Thank you very much anyway," I said. "But first of all, I don't want to offend him and secondly, when I say $550 I mean delivered, out the door, no payments. I know what I can do."

"Please come with me and talk to the manager." she invited.

I reluctantly followed her to the little office that was set up in the trailer. She directed me to sit down while she let the manager know I was there.

I sat. I began to pray. "Lord, You know this would be a dream come true to have this piano. You also know that I

164

promised not to go into debt. If there's any way this piano could be mine, I thank You. If not, I know the day will come. As I sat there my faith began to grow. I started thinking, God is the One who directed me here. Why would He direct me here if I weren't going to get a piano? My prayer changed, I started thanking Him for the piano.

A few moments later the manager came out. I repeated the same story to him that I had told the salesgirl. He looked at me and said, "Where do we need to deliver it?" I was ecstatic. As I got in the car and headed home, the Lord said to me, This is your graduation gift from Me." This reminded me of the verse in James 1:17 KJV that says, *Every good gift and every perfect gift is from above, and cometh down from the Father of lights ....*

A graduation gift from my Father in heaven! He was the One Who helped me get my Doctor of Ministry and Chaplain's Board Certification—both miracles in themselves. I was mystified and beside myself with gratitude.

But this isn't the end of my piano stories. Twelve years later when I got married it meant a move from California to New Hampshire. My husband told me I would not be able to bring my piano with me; that there was no room in his house and he had a keyboard I could play. I didn't want to play keyboard. I love the piano. He said we would look for a small upright once we were settled, but really there was no room or place in his home for one. Ten years went by and still no piano. My Father in heaven knowing my heart surprised me with my third piano.

When we purchased our home in Florida, we were deciding where we would place furniture. I pointed to one wall and said to my husband, "This is where our upright is going to go. Before you hang the pictures please go online and find the height of an upright piano." So he did.

Several months later a new neighbor knocked at the door bringing with her another neighbor who I had not yet met. "I just wanted Sarah to see your home." I welcomed them in.

As I was showing them around we came to the place designated for our upright piano. I explained the plan. Sarah smiled and said, "Oh, you want a piano?"

"Are you kidding?" I said. "I've been praying for a piano for ten years. I can't play well, but I used to love to play and sing songs of worship during my devotional time."

"I have a piano you can have." she offered."

"Are you serious? I would love it. How much do you want for it?"

"I don't want anything for it. I just want you to take it and enjoy it."

"If you're getting rid of your piano you have just found a home for it!" I said.

"Good. We'll figure out how to get it over here. In fact, I have a guitar and ukulele that I will throw in with it if you want them."

"You're sure? That would be wonderful. My husband and son both play the guitar and my grandson plays the ukulele. When they visit we can have a sing-along! I would be happy to have them if that helps you, too."

That night as I lay in bed excited about my new piano suddenly the thought occurred to me, 'Oh no, what if it's battered and beaten like the first one I got? My husband will not be happy with me. I became nervous. I had been quick to accept it sight unseen.

A few days later, after renting some piano dollies, we rolled the piano across the street and settled it into its chosen spot. Once again God had heard my prayers. This time I was gifted with a beautiful black Baldwin upright piano with a lovely tone, tuned perfectly by Sarah's son, a piano tuner. The pictures the Lord had helped us pick out and had us place above where the piano would live, brought the whole room together with their shiny black, browns and green tones.

Love Overflowed:

Now once again I can play and sing praises to my King. My heart thrills every time I sit down on the bench and place my fingers on the keyboard. Thank You Jesus again, for the third time, Your exorbitant love gift to me—another piano!

The Bible says in Psalm 37:4, *Delight yourself also in the LORD, and He shall give you the desires of your heart.* And so He has—three pianos from my Father. And I will pour out my love and gratitude singing praises of thanksgiving.

What heart desire do you want to put before God? Are you willing to wait if necessary?

You crown the year with your bounty, and your carts overflow with abundance.—Psalm 65:11 NIV.

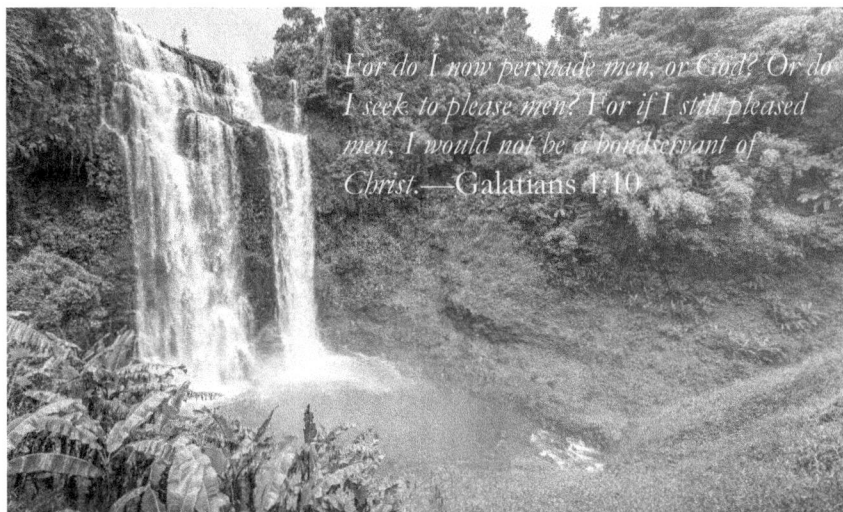

For do I now persuade men, or God? Or do I seek to please men? For if I still pleased men, I would not be a bondservant of Christ. —Galatians 1:10

To Hug Or Not To Hug

When I was a young woman, I was a real people-pleaser. I lived a long way away from my biological family. At that time we didn't have a close union of love for Jesus, Christianity or a living faith. Nothing really held our family together. I was a relatively new Christian so the church was my family. They just didn't know it yet. But I knew it. When I came into the church I came in with gusto!

Since my nature is to be a hugger, I attacked everybody. Hello—hug, hello—hug, hello—hug. I soon learned not everybody is a hugger. Now, I am much more respectful. I can generally pick up on the boundaries people put up. But when I was younger and more naive I would gregariously hug everybody.

One day at church a well-meaning older couple took me by the arm and said, "Honey, can you come over here? We need to talk to you. Your behavior is just not exemplary of a Christian woman! You shouldn't be hugging everyone like you do." Scripture says in Ephesians 5:15-16 NIV, *Be very careful, then, how you live—not as unwise but as wise, making the most of every opportunity ...*

With Love Overflowing

I'm very teachable and respect the wisdom of those who are more mature than I am. These were older, wiser people and I listened with both ears. They continued, "Derry, you're not conducting yourself like a Christian woman."

"I'm not?"

They went on to tell me I shouldn't be hugging like I was hugging and it really was not acceptable. I was devastated because I had just fallen in love with Jesus. I had learned that He is a God of love. There was nothing in the whole world I wanted more than to reflect Christ's character in my life. I felt like I had totally defamed Him. I went home and I cried and then I determined I was going to do much better. (I later learned the proper way for a woman to hug a man—not related—is from the side, not full front on.)

I respected the counsel of this older couple so after that I just went to church and said, "Hello" and attempted to keep my hands to myself. However, I made an amazing discovery. When my hands stop working so does my mouth. Pretty soon I was hardly saying anything at all. After about two months of "good behavior" I found myself increasingly depressed.

One day after church as I was home resting, lying on my bed, I was contemplating with the Lord. "Father, I don't understand why I feel so low. I just feel rather depressed. I don't know what's wrong with me. What happened to my joy?" Tears moistened my cheeks.

It was as though I could feel God's presence so close, almost lovingly chuckling at me, saying, "Oh Derry, be who I created you to be. You can reach people others can never reach and they will reach people you can never reach. Be who I created you to be!"

All of a sudden I felt free. The Lord set me free! Unchained! Free to be me, for my God. He wants us not to be people pleasers, but servants of the living God. That's what He tells us in Galatians 1:10 ESV, *For am I now seeking the ap-*

proval of man, or of God? Or am I trying to please man? If I were still trying to please man, I would not be a servant of Christ. and in 1 Peter 2:15, *For this is the will of God, that by doing good you may put to silence the ignorance of foolish men.*

Freedom from having to live up to others expectations and being accountable only to God allows us peace and holy boldness. It gives us the freedom to try new things when God calls us to do them without concern of failure.

Can you imagine what this poor little couple must have thought? They had talked to me and I had been so good. They thought they had done their job; then all of a sudden, two months later I'm back at it again! Oh dear.

The Lord desires our joy be full. He made us each uniquely different and wonderful and beautiful in His eyes. There is no one in the whole world who could fill our place with Him.

Maybe He's asking us to sit home and be intercessory prayer partners. Maybe He's put us on the telephone committee. Maybe He decided we're supposed to speak up front or He has gifted us with musical talent, or given us a servant's heart to do church janitorial. Whatever it is God calls us to do, He never, never, never, never will ask us to do anything without empowering us to do it. And once we realize that, we get a little gutsy. We get a Holy boldness if we know God is asking us to do something and we'll move forward with whatever it is.

Many years later I had another "hug" incident. I was meeting two of my cousins for the first time. Both girls were a couple of years older. I immediately lunged towards them with my arms open. One of the girls responded with a big hug. The other put her hand out indicating "stop." "I am not a hugger," she informed.

I laughed and countered, "No worries. I have a lot of other ways I can hug. I could even hug you through a card." We were instantly friends!

171

With Love Overflowing

Someone once said, "We are to make people feel comfortable and let the Holy Spirit make them feel uncomfortable. We can do that best by being a transparent Christian, the unique person God created us to be, filling the position for which we alone were created and loving others with His love.

Love Overflowed:

God saw my tears and spoke words of loving affirmation to me—to be myself—not a version of what someone wanted me to be. To hug or not to hug—that was the question.

You did not choose Me, but I chose you and appointed you that you should go and bear fruit, and that your fruit should remain, that whatever you ask the Father in My name He may give you.—John 15:16.

Are you living to please others, to live up to their expectations? Are you being uniquely you? If not, claim the promise in Galatians 1:10 to not be a people-pleaser but a servant of the living God. Our God Who created you uniquely you doesn't want you to compromise who you are to please someone else—but He does want you to continue to grow and mature being transformed into His character!

Tsunami

Raising a family of seven children and then accepting other children to live with you too, doesn't leave much time for additions to your calendar. You develop a sense of satisfaction for just making it through the day successfully without having to do damage control.

When I found myself alone, I decided I needed some recoup time. Going away for a vacation with my mother was something we hadn't done since I was a small child living at home. I had been given a timeshare opportunity in Acapulco. Why not? Neither of us had ever been there. It might be fun. It would certainly remove us from all the pressures we were surrounded with. We needed a break and we needed time together!

I gave the invitation and Mom agreed. Arrangements made, we began getting things together in anticipation of an adventure. We got more than we had bargained for!

When mom and I got together we would laugh a lot. It didn't take much. Both of us are friendly and draw others into our circle easily.

With Love Overflowing

While waiting to board our flight we made new friends. In no time we had a number of people participating in our conversation, laughing and sharing life.

By the time we boarded the plane we were near hysterics, we had been laughing so hard. We saw the concern on the faces of the flight attendants when we embarked, which made us laugh all the more. To them, we looked like trouble. You could see on their faces that they thought we had already had too much to drink and wondered if we were going to calm down or become rowdy. Little did they know we had been drinking something stronger than liquor. We drank something strong enough to float a battleship—water!

Of course we did settle down and were respectful of the flight attendants and other passengers, but we had already made our mark. Everyone wanted to be by us because we were happy, fun, and caring. Yes, caring. We expressed interest in others and what was going on in their lives.

Usually people would share their hearts and we would end up ministering to them and praying with them. This was no exception. Mom and I were a fun and effective team.

We arrived at a beautiful resort and quickly settled in. It was early enough and hot enough to go out and get in the pool. This became a daily event for us. Go to the pool, swim and relax, have the waiters come by and ask what we wanted to drink. We always asked for a virgin Piña Colada thinking that we were being health conscious while getting our exercise. However it didn't enter our mind how fattening a Piña Colada might be—especially several a day due to the heat. In that week we both gained significant weight, unfortunately.

We thought we were settling into a great routine, but little did we know what was on the horizon ... or coming across the horizon. It was our second day there, around 9:45pm. Mom wanted something cold to drink so I went down to the restaurant to get her something. When I came back she was tucked in bed watching the 10:00 news.

Her first words to me were, "There's a tsunami on its way here."

Mom always ready for a gag wasn't going to suck me in at 10:15 at night. I was ready for bed. "Yeah right, Mom. Good try. I'm not falling for that one."

"I'm not joking. Come in here and listen to the news. They just announced it. It's on its way up the coast and this is one of the targeted spots where they expect it to hit."

I stopped and just looked at her. Something in her tone said she wasn't kidding and my head started spinning. "You're really not kidding?" I asked. I started praying—for everyone's safety, for wisdom and for the storm to subside so the tsunami would dissipate. We were staying right on the coast. We could walk out the door to the beach and play in the ocean.

"No, I'm not Dee. What are we going to do?"

"I haven't waited 20 years to go on a vacation with you just to lose you in a tsunami, I'll tell you that much. Let me think—let's pray." We claimed the promise in Isaiah 26:3, *You will keep* him *in perfect peace,* Whose *mind is stayed* on You, *Because he trusts in You.* and also asked for wisdom to know what to do.

I decided that since we had time to prepare and since no one at the resort was warning us yet, I would go down to the desk and ask if there were any rental cars available anywhere close.

When I asked, their response was, "Where would you want to go at this hour of the night? It's after 11:00. It's not safe for you to be out now." By their attitude I sensed I would be stuck unless I told them everything. I thought of the text in Psalm 46:10, *Be still, and know that I* am *God;* but it seemed to me that the "be still" part was more about sharing and then waiting without pressuring, than to be quiet about what I knew.

I could really play this story up and give you a blow-by-blow report of what happened and what the responses were, but in short, they countered with, "What? There hasn't been a tsunami here for over 30 years!"

I created an alarm. I admitted that because of my mother's age and agility, I was trying to make arrangements before panic hit the other guests.

Within 30 minutes they had arranged a room for us at a hotel way up the mountain about 30 minutes away and a taxi that would be arriving in about 15 minutes. It would cost me but it was worth it.

I rushed back to the room. Mom and I started packing our things and were ready to go when the taxi arrived. Despite the fact that things had happened relatively quickly, it was after 1:00 when we finally got to our room. We were exhausted but grateful. We turned on the TV for an update. The first words we heard were, "The tsunami warning has been cancelled."

We just looked at each other and shook our heads. Then we thanked the Lord for intervening. We would return to the resort the next day. It had already been paid for—this room wasn't.

As I lay in bed that night (morning actually) I thought, if there were another warning tomorrow, would I do the same thing again? Yes, I would. When we receive a warning, we have two choices; we can heed it and take action, or ignore it and pretend everything is alright.

Jesus gives us many warnings and opportunities in the Bible. He also promises He will not do anything without letting His people know. That's reassuring! But to receive His warnings, we have to be in tune with Him and study His word.

But this I call to mind, and therefore I have hope: The steadfast love of the LORD never ceases, his mercies never come to an end; they are new every morning; great is thy faithfulness. "The LORD is my portion," says my soul, "therefore I will hope in him." The LORD is good to those who wait for him, to the soul that seeks him. It is good that one should wait quietly for the salvation of the LORD.—Lamentations 3:21-26 RSV.

We've heard for a long time that Jesus is coming again and time is short; but if you read scripture you will see we are on the very brink of Jesus' return. Prophecy is being fulfilled all around us in this world and there is no excuse for us not to be ready.

Just like my vacation with Mom and having to pack up and leave our room—it may be inconvenient to follow God's warning. It may even cost us something. But better we heed the warning than get caught in the "storm."

No matter what is ahead, Jesus is the way. He will care for His children and provide what they need for the situation at hand. It may not be easy. No one said that following Jesus would be easy, but one thing we know for sure, we have a home in heaven waiting for us.

Love Overflowed:

Thank You Father for the warning, and for providing a "safe" room for us. Thank You especially for answering our prayers and dissipating the tsunami. Your love assures us that You have a place prepared for us and that we will see You soon. Blessed be the name of the Lord.

In my Father's house are many rooms; if it were not so, would I have told you that I go to prepare a place for you? And when I go and prepare a place for you, I will come again and will take you to myself, that where I am you may be also.—John 14:2-3 RSV.

Have you secured your home in heaven by securing your heart in Jesus? What warning messages or signs are you disregarding? What do you need to do to prepare for an emergency? Claim the promise in 2 Timothy 1:7, *For God has not given us a spirit of fear, but of power and of love and of a sound mind.* Talk to God. Use your head and be prepared before an emergency strikes!

In Him We Live And Move And Have Our Being
—Helen Steiner Rice†

We walk in a world that is strange and unknown,
And in the midst of the crowd we still feel alone.
We question our purpose, our part and our place
In this vast land of mystery suspended in space.
We probe and explore and try hard to explain
The tumult of thoughts that our minds entertain …
But all of our probings and complex explanations
Of man's inner feelings and fears and frustrations
Still leave us engulfed in the "MYSTERY of LIFE"
With all of its struggles and suffering and strife,
Unable to fathom what tomorrow will bring—
But there is one truth to which we can cling,
For while LIFE's a MYSTERY man can't understand
The "GREAT GIVER OF LIFE" is holding our hand
And safe in HIS care there is no need for seeing
For "IN HIM WE LIVE and MOVE and HAVE OUR BEING."

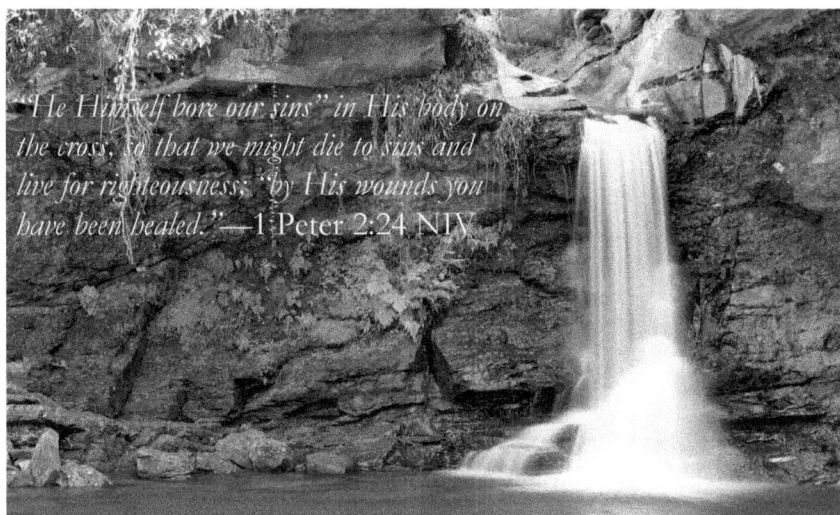

"He Himself bore our sins" in His body on the cross, so that we might die to sins and live for righteousness; "by His wounds you have been healed."—1 Peter 2:24 NIV

Two For Jesus

No two days are alike ministering as a hospital chaplain. Before I go on duty I pray that God will help me make a difference for His Kingdom's glory. During my devotional time I ask God to help me with a time of heart-searching, confession, repentance and cleansing from all unrighteousness. Then I ask that He would help me have a sweet and humble spirit that responds to His voice and responds to the needs around me. I asked Him to guide me to those who have a responsive heart and give me the words to speak to them.

This particular day I was scheduled to work in the Emergency Room of a large metropolitan hospital. I had been on duty several hours. The Emergency Room was full.

As I stepped into a patient's room to make a report to the nurse, a cheery voice from the bed greeted me. "Hi." I turned to find a man in his 40s smiling at me.

"What are you doing here?" I asked.

"Alcohol," he responded.

"Why?" I questioned.

"I don't know. I love God. I have a wonderful Christian wife and two great children. I don't know. I just can't break the habit."

I thought of the verse in Isaiah 24:9 KJV, *They shall not drink wine with a song; strong drink shall be bitter to them that drink it.* I sat down next to his bed and asked, "Do you want to break the habit?"

"Oh yes, but I just can't."

We prayed. Then I took out a piece of paper and drew a cross. Just as Pastor Paul Coneff had taught me I began going through the story of Christ from Gethsemane to the crucifixion. I asked the patient to explain in contemporary terminology how he thought Jesus felt and what kind of abuse He had suffered. As we progressed with the story he identified verbal, physical, sexual, emotional, religious, psychological and satanic abuse.

We came to the part of the story where Jesus said, "I thirst."

"Do you remember what they offered Him?" I asked.

"I think it was vinegar and myrrh," he answered.

"Right! Vinegar or sour wine and myrrh on a hyssop stick. Do you know why they offered it to Him?

"No."

"They offered it to Him to numb the pain. Did Jesus drink it?"

"No. I don't think so."

"That's right! Mark 15:23 says, *Then they gave Him wine mingled with myrrh to drink, but He did not take it.* It was a numbing agent, an anesthetic. And it was at that very moment that Jesus conquered addictions for all people. Any addiction is about numbing pain and Jesus refused to have his body and mind numbed from pain.

The patient began to weep. He said, "I never believed that Jesus really understood. Now I know He does."

We talked a while longer and then had prayer, asking God to give him courage to resist the attacks of the enemy and break the hold the devil had over him. He confessed his sins and asked Jesus to take over his life. He seemed hopeful.

I was about to leave when a young voice on the other side of the curtain called to me. He had overheard my conversation. This 15-year-old boy had been transported by ambulance from his high school because he also suffered from alcohol abuse and had been heavily intoxicated.

This young man had heard me share about the suffering of our Lord and the redemption we have in Jesus; how He died to pay the penalty of our sins that we might have life eternal. "I want Jesus to help me, too. I want to pray, too. I don't want to live this way any more. I repent before the Lord."

He had never been to church and he didn't know anything about Jesus until now. But with all his heart he embraced the message he had just heard. After praying and sharing, he took off his bandana, the symbol of his gang, and threw it in the trash.

Because your heart was responsive and you humbled yourself before the LORD when you heard what I have spoken against this place and its people—that they would become accursed and laid waste—and because you tore your robes and wept in my presence, I also have heard you, declares the LORD.—2 Kings 22:19 NIV.

Together we discussed how he would explain to his very angry parents the transformation that had happened during this hospital visit. Before I left, I assured him, "God's power will be imparted as you depend on Him."

When I am afraid, I put my trust in thee. In God, whose word I praise, in God I trust without a fear. What can flesh do to me?
—Psalm 56:3-4 RSV.

With Love Overflowing

Before my eyes I experienced a young man respond, repent, and humble himself before the Lord. God in exchange gave him peace of mind and a peaceful countenance. I'm convinced there is more to the story, which I will find out someday in heaven.

Jesus says in Revelation 3:20 KJV, *Behold, I stand at the door, and knock: if any man hear my voice, and open the door, I will come in to him, and will sup with him, and he with me.*

Jesus stands at the door and knocks. We have to let Him in. He instructs, we must obey. The Bible says in Hebrews 3:7-8 NIV, … *Today if you hear His voice, do not harden your hearts* … Jesus invites in Matthew 11:28, *Come to Me all* you *who labor and are heavy laden, and I will give you rest.* When we respond, we are revitalized. Come and rest.

Love Overflowed:

God planned patient visitations unexpected to me because in His great love for them He knew He had prepared me to break their bondages in Jesus' name. Two more for Jesus, secured for the Kingdom.

… *taste and see that the* LORD *is good;* …—Psalm 34:8.

Have you asked Jesus into your life? Have you invited Him to take full control? How will He use you today to reach someone else and let them know of Jesus' love for them?

He is your praise, and He is your God, who has done for you these great and awesome things which your eyes have seen.—Deuteronomy 10:21

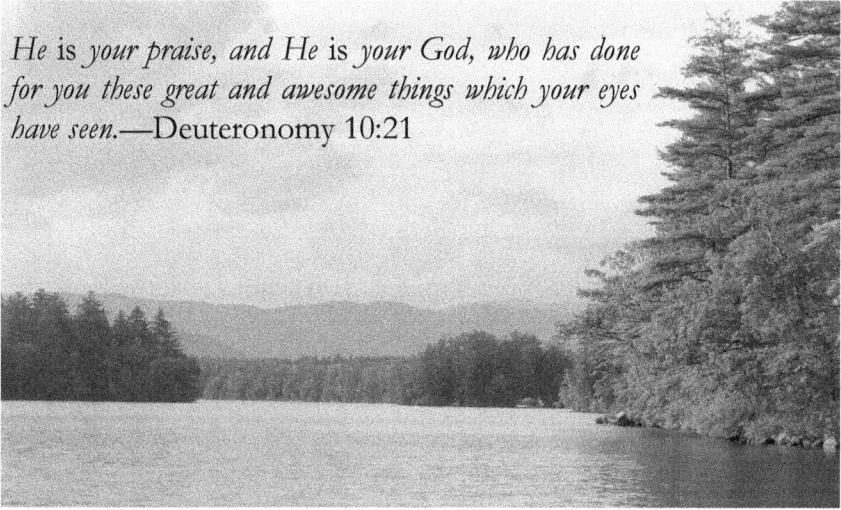

Valentine's Day

When I was alone for 12 years, God had some innovative ways of showing me He loved me. A number of them were very unexpected. But I love surprises!

One way He consistently surprised me was on Valentine's Day. If you've read my book *With Gladness Every Day*, you might remember the story about God bringing me flowers. Even today when I get unexpected flowers, I consider them a 'kiss from heaven.' To me they're a way of God expressing His love, and reminding me He is aware of me and everything concerning me.

On Valentine's Day He has used His people to bless me with lovely bouquets of flowers and sometimes candy. Of course I also realize these are loving gifts from the people who gave them to me, but I could sense God behind their gifts.

One very special Valentine's Day I received a phone call. The voice at the other end said, "Congratulations! You have won this year's Valentines gift."

"What?" I said. "Who is this calling and how could I have won a Valentine's gift?"

"Is your name Derry?"

With Love Overflowing

"It is."

"Then you have won the Valentine's gift this year. We would like to know where to deliver it."

I asked, "Is this a joke?"

"Absolutely not. We would like to deliver it this afternoon if that works out for you."

"Sure that would be fine. Do you want to tell me what it is?"

"We'd rather surprise you."

"Fine. I'll see you at my house in a couple of hours."

After we hung up, it was as though I could sense God chuckling. He had a love gift for me, again! A few hours later a six-foot heart-shaped balloon made to look like a hot-air balloon with a basket hanging from it and a banner attached that said "Love is in the Air" made its appearance at my door. The basket was filled with flowers, candy, gifts and a stuffed teddy bear. A Happy Valentine's Day from Jesus.

Love Overflowed:

God is such a fun companion, providing for my needs, anticipating my longings, bringing me surprise love gifts. Thank you again, Jesus. I love Valentine's Day, because I love how You love me with Your surprises!!!

For you are great and do marvelous deeds; you alone are God.
                    —Psalm 86:10 NIV.

Are you aware that God creatively pursues His children? He enjoys pouring His love out on you. Do you notice His efforts?

184

Now therefore, fear the LORD, serve Him in sincerity and in truth, . . .
— Joshua 24:14

Weddings Aren't Marriages

This is a very difficult story to write. It is also the last story that is being written for this book. I thought the book was finished, but God has been prompting me to put this story together. I am writing it, not only because I sense God directing me to, but also because I believe in marriage— despite the fact that I have been divorced. I'm writing it because I am aware of so many hurting marriages, and the heartache carried that instills within one the inclination to give up. My prayer is that my transparency in this story will in some way resonate with you who need to hear my testimony and give you hope and determination to hang on. Solutions will come more quickly if God is first in your life.

Costa Rica is an incredibly beautiful place. I never would have guessed that I would one day have an opportunity to visit there, but that is where my husband planned our honeymoon and I was delighted. I knew very

little about Costa Rica at that time, but information came in quickly. My marriage to him meant I would be leaving California, my family, friends, job at the hospital that I loved and the community that I had become a part of. All were dear to my heart.

One of the first things I learned about Costa Rica came from a question we were asked by one of the hospital staff. She said, "How cool! You're going to Costa Rica. Are you going to go on the zip lines while you're there?"

My soon-to-be husband quickly stated, "Absolutely."

After she left my office, I asked him, "What is a zip line?"

In the middle of his explanation, someone else came in to tell me goodbye and asked the same question. But he continued by saying he had been there and had gone on the zip line. "It was great! We were up about 250 feet above the trees."

When I heard that, the first thought in my head was, *nobody is getting me on a zip line!* Having developed some sense of savvy, I kept that information to myself. I know that sometimes people talk but don't always follow through. I hoped that would be the case with us. I would wait this one out and address it when and if I needed to.

It was several days later when we arrived in Costa Rica. The wedding was behind us—so was the move from California to New Hampshire. I was tired but looking forward to the reprieve and the opportunity to have some fun and togetherness with my new husband. Boy was I in for a surprise.

As we landed and headed for a taxi to take us to our hotel, my husband said, "Donna would have loved it here." (Donna was his late wife of 43 years.) My heart began to sink.

186

Would Donna be accompanying us on our honeymoon too? That was only the beginning. At meals he began to cry because she wasn't there. We would start a meal and he would leave me sitting there alone because he needed to excuse himself to go cry. I held my tongue.

Let no corrupt word proceed out of your mouth, but what is good for necessary edification, that it may impart grace to the hearers.
—Ephesians 4:29.

Hour after hour and day after day it continued. I wondered what I was doing there and why he had married me. Things weren't getting any better. Almost every conversation was about Donna. We had a few brief moments of communication and then he would lapse back into his "Donna" world. I hadn't even been given an opportunity to prove myself to be a potentially good wife, or even an acceptable one at best. The odds seemed stacked against me. I felt like I was in a triangle—like a mistress tagging along hoping for some recognition.

About the fourth day he announced we would be going to try out a zip line. He just needed to find where one was. I didn't say anything. We spoke very little, unless it was about Donna. I was falling into depression and despair. I had left a job I loved, all of my family and friends ... for this? Had I really heard God correctly? Had He really called me to marry this man? Maybe going on a zip line wasn't a bad idea. Right about now I didn't care if I fell off the zip line.

He found a place and we got geared up. I lost all fear. Right now death seemed like it would be a sweet release. I might as well enjoy it—throw myself into it.

And I did. I had a great time! I even rappelled down

the 70-foot rope. And I survived the whole experience. Now what? I survived this adventure, but how would I survive my new life?

There is no fear in love; but perfect love casts out fear, because fear involves torment. But he who fears has not been made perfect in love.
 —1 John 4:18.

I have learned that people who have been happily married for a long time often have a very difficult time adjusting to remarriage. They don't want to be alone. They want another companion. But as soon as they "tie the knot" they begin to feel guilty—feel like they are betraying their deceased spouse. If they start to get over their guilt, their children are there to remind them and ask them "How could you do this?" Any bad or difficult times they went through before are forgotten and their late spouse is elevated to a pedestal. Often the new spouse becomes rejected—abandoned. Things go downhill pretty fast. The rejected spouse becomes disillusioned with their life and the future looks bleak—hopeless. The "guilty" spouse isolates. The new spouse "treads water."

Marriages late in life often find that even if things are good between the couple, they are sometimes complicated by adult children from their previous marriage. The children feel like their parent is being replaced and they are protective of their memory. Their hearts are not open to accept this intruder. They may be busy living their own lives and don't have time to care for or reach out to the now alone and grieving parent, but instead of being happy that their parent has found someone to love who loves them, they interfere with the relationship growing or establishing something beautiful and special of its own.

On the flip side, there are those marriages where they are so thrilled that God would give them someone again, they treat them like they are a treasure. They introduce them to their children in just that way and they are accepted and loved right into the family. It seems to me, this is the way it should be with Christians. We should have enough love to share. We should be able to love with a different kind of love for each person God brings into our lives. No one will ever take the place of the one that has left us, but the newcomer should be loved for who they are … if we are willing to look for the good and not the negative, and give them a chance.

Do not remember the former things, Nor consider the things of old. Behold, I will do a new thing, Now it shall spring forth; Shall you not know it? …—Isaiah 43:18-19.

That wasn't my experience and I was devastated. If I had not known in my heart that this was God's plan, I would have given up … literally packed my bags and left, but I believe in marriage. I believe in keeping my word … sticking it out. I believe that God has a plan, even if I don't understand, and that the end of the story hasn't yet been told. I really believed that we were together to partnership in ministry and be an effective duo for God and the glory of the kingdom.

As we think, so we are. The reality of who we are is determined by our thoughts and the inclinations of our hearts. Our words and actions follow accordingly. Proverbs 23:7 says, *For as he thinks in his heart, so is he* …. We determine our own futures by the way we respond to life and the choices we make.

When I know that God has called me, I will follow that calling no matter what—despite personal pain or loss. At this time in my life, there was a great conflict raging within me. One day I was praising God, the next day questioning or giving up. God knew my heart struggles and was with me.

Where is God when your heart is broken and you feel like giving up? He is right by your side. Do you always feel Him there? No. But He is there. He finds ways to pour out love and encouragement. God is love.

189

With Love Overflowing

   Some people will turn to puppies and kittens when they are alone or lonely. Unconditional love is returned from pets. They are patient and loyal. There is comfort in holding something alive and cuddly in your arms. The love you are longing for is reciprocated in a small way by an animal looking for its needs to be met and by responding to your overtures of affection.

   I didn't have a pet. I was in Costa Rica, feeling terribly alone. So God sent me friends of nature—coatimundis! Are you asking, "What in the world is a coatimundi?" They are called coati for short. They can be seen all over the country of Costa Rica. They look similar to a raccoon. They are carnivores that eat insects, fruit, nuts and eggs. They are also scavengers. They are very social and travel in groups. They associate humans with food so they don't seem to be afraid around us and can become very aggressive.

   In the midst of my sorrow and aloneness there in Costa Rica, God sent me a whole big family of coatimundis. I sat down in the grass and began to feed them. It probably wasn't the smartest thing I've ever done, but it was "a moment" in the midst of heartache—a distraction. My husband just shook his head when I sat down on the grass, told me I shouldn't be doing that and then left. The small group that I started with turned into more than I could count running out of the jungle towards me. It was time to leave and I made a hasty getaway, but I had nowhere to run. I didn't want to go back to our room. I didn't know where to go.

casting all your care upon Him, for He cares for you. Be sober, be vigilant; because your adversary the devil walks about like a roaring lion, seeking whom he may devour.—1 Peter 5:7-8.

God sent a distraction from my heartache by sending the coatis. He also gave me other people who needed prayer—who needed a caring presence. It helps when you go outside of yourself and look for other hurting people you can come along side of. I wanted to hide, but instead I sang a song of praise in my heart for the things I could be thankful for—His love, another day of life, and my family on the west coast. Then I sought out others.

If satan can keep us in a hopeless state and isolate us from others, he can steal from us the opportunity to minister to others and win them to Jesus. Resist him!!!

I didn't know how to break through my husband's grief. He didn't know what to do with me. Our honeymoon, our marriage, was a façade. It took years of hard work and determination from both of us, but we stuck it out and are thankful we did. We enjoy each other, and the friendship and intimacy we have come to experience. Our love and commitment for each other has grown; so has the fun we share. God put us together for a reason and the enemy wanted none of it! Don't let the enemy have you miss out either. **Your choices affect your future.** The verse in James 4:7 RSV comes to mind: *Submit yourselves therefore to God. Resist the devil and he will flee from you.* There is power in God's promises—if we claim them and apply them to our lives.

In order to make marriage work, you have to have some basic values—principles that you are determined to live out in your life. They are listed here, just as God shared them with me one morning before we taught a marriage education class. Then He helped me find the scripture verses—Bible promises to claim as my own for fulfillment in my life.

- Be a person of integrity—keep your word.
  Philippians 4:13, *I can do all things through Christ who strengthens me.*

- Be a person of integrity—be trustworthy. Don't lie.
  Proverbs 12:22, *Lying lips* are *an abomination to the* LORD, *But those who deal truthfully* are *His delight.*

191

With Love Overflowing

- Be willing to be made willing.
  Mark 9:24, ... *Lord, I believe; help my unbelief!*

- Put others before self.
  Philippians 2:3, Let *nothing* be done *through selfish ambition or conceit, but in lowliness of mind let each esteem others better than himself.*

- Look for the good in each other.

- Allow yourself to be open to give love and accept love.

- Pay attention to how you communicate.
  Ephesians 4:29-32 *Let no corrupt word proceed out of your mouth, but what is good for necessary edification, that it may impart grace to the hearers. And do not grieve the Holy Spirit of God, by whom you were sealed for the day of redemption. Let all bitterness, wrath, anger, clamor, and evil speaking be put away from you, with all malice. And be kind to one another, tenderhearted, forgiving one another, even as God in Christ forgave you.*

  Proverbs 18:21 *Death and life* are *in the power of the tongue,* ...

  Proverbs 16:27-28, *An ungodly man digs up evil, And it is on his lips like a burning fire. A perverse man sows strife, And a whisperer separates the best of friends.*

- Stop living in the past and embrace the future. I didn't say forget the past—memories are important.
  Ecclesiastes 7:10, *Do not say, "Why were the former days better than these?" For you do not inquire wisely concerning this."*
  Isaiah 43:18-19, *Do not remember the former things, Nor consider the things of old. Behold, I will do a new thing, Now it shall spring forth; Shall you not know it?* ...

Luke 9:62, *But Jesus said to him, "No one, having put his hand to the plow, and looking back, is fit for the kingdom of God.*

2 Corinthians 5:17, *Therefore, if anyone is in Christ, he is a new creation; old things have passed away; behold, all things have become new.*

- Forgive
  Matthew 6:14-15, *For if you forgive men their trespasses, your heavenly Father will also forgive you. But if you do not forgive men their trespasses, neither will your Father forgive your trespasses.*

If you find loving and forgiving difficult, pray "God help me love with Your love and forgive with Your forgiveness."

Remember that marriage vows are a covenant, not a contract. What is the difference? I found a great list on UpCounsel.com that I want to share with you. It is worth meditating on:

- A Contract is legally binding. A Covenant is a spiritual agreement.

- A Contract is an agreement between parties which can be broken. A Covenant is a pledge, a perpetual promise.

- You sign a Contract. You seal a Covenant

- A Contract is a mutually beneficial relationship. A Covenant is something you fulfill.

- A Contract exchanges one good for another. A Covenant is giving oneself to the other.

- You can opt out of a Contract. A Covenant is about having the strength to hold up your part of the promise.

With Love Overflowing

- One can stop paying in a Contract when one party is not fulfilling their part in a deal. In a Covenant, the party not getting their needs met supports the failing party so that they can meet their obligations. You must hold up your promise even if the other does not hold up their pledge.

- Contracts are enforceable by the courts. Covenants depend on your values. Covenants are trust-based promises that rely on your integrity and discipline.

So then, they are no longer two but one flesh. Therefore what God has joined together, let not man separate.—Matthew 19:6.

The bottom line is this: Life is tough. Relationships can be difficult and challenging. But if we are determined to live for Jesus and put Him first in all things, he will give us the heart, the determination, the direction and the wisdom.

Jesus loves you, this I know. He will never leave you or forsake you. He loves you with an everlasting, incomprehensible, overwhelming, extravagant, unrelenting, exorbitant love, a love that no human being can take the place of. When you know Jesus' love, nothing else matters except to please Him and honor Him in the way you live and the choices you make.

Your heart's desire will be to not break His heart and to pour out your love to those in your circle with His love. To bring Him delight will fill you with unspeakable joy. That's a clue that your love for Him has so grown that Jesus has become irresistible!

His love will overflow in all you do. His unrelenting love will see you through. You will have peace in the midst of the storm. You will have an unshakeable goal of eternity and spending your forever with Him. Nothing in this life will supersede your desire to be with Jesus. You will be able to show others mercy and grace because Jesus has shown it to you. You will be able to pour out love, compassion and tender care even when it isn't reciprocated because you understand what your Savior suffered for you. You know that your heartache doesn't even compare to His heartache and suffering. You will remember that His word says in 1 John 4:20, *If someone says, "I love God," and hates his brother, he is a liar; for he who does not love his brother whom he has seen, how can he love God whom he has not seen?*

Jesus gave His all. We need to follow His example in all things. Have I? No. Do I wish I had? Yes. Would my life have been different? Absolutely. I can't unring the bell, but I can learn from my mistakes, do things differently and keep my eyes focused on Jesus my Lord, the One Who truly loves and loves truly—unconditionally and without reservation.

I have been crucified with Christ; it is no longer I who live, but Christ who lives in me; and the life *which I now live in the flesh I live by faith in the Son of God, who loved me and gave Himself for me.*
—Galatians 2:20 RSV.

Be sober, be watchful. Your adversary the devil prowls around like a roaring lion, seeking some one to devour. Resist him, firm in your faith, ...
—1 Peter 5:8-9 RSV.

Satan desperately tries to convince us we're not enough and that our life doesn't make a difference. We are in a spiritual battle but God has already won. We know the end of this story. It is written in the scriptures. We can be confident of our victory because our Lord Jesus was victorious.

We can trust and apply the promises of God for our lives and have the same success Jesus had. He knew His empowerment and direction came from spending time with His Father and in receiving the daily infilling/baptism of the Holy Spirit. Be confident. Strengthen your resolve.

... choose for yourselves this day whom you will serve,—Joshua 24:15.

To Whom will you give your allegiance, your love with full surrender? When we put our Lord Jesus first, we become transformed. We are a new creation. We can do whatever we need to do and be whoever we need to be because He will enable us. He gives us instruction in His word how to most effectively bring health to our marriage. If you feel you are always the one giving in or soothing the wounds, stand in faith. Proverbs 18:22 RSV says, *He who finds a wife finds a good thing, and obtains favor from the LORD.* Let your confession be: "My husband has found a good thing and I am that good thing." Then do what you need to do to be that "good thing" with God's help. If you had a good thing and you no longer do ... ask yourself what you did to contribute to the change.

In Ephesians 5:21-28 NLT God gives the married couple His unfailing counsel, *And further,* **submit to one another out of reverence for Christ. For wives, this means submit to your husbands** *as to the Lord. For a husband is the head of his wife as Christ is the head of the church. He is the Savior of his body, the church. As the church submits to Christ, so you wives should submit to your husbands in everything. For* **husbands, this means love your wives,** *just as Christ loved the church. He gave up his life for her to make her holy and clean, washed by the cleansing of God's word. He did this to present her to himself as a glorious church without a spot or wrinkle or any other blemish. Instead, she will be holy and without fault. In* *the same way, husbands ought to love their wives as they love their own bodies. For a man who loves his wife actually shows love for himself.*

This text gives such definite direction. Husbands are admonished to love their wives and wives are admonished to respect their husbands. Have you given that much thought?

Men, when a woman feels loved and we feel we're the most important thing in the world to our man, we will do almost anything for him. When we feel loved, it makes it so much easier to show our man respect, even though we know respect is not optional. Love is expressed as a commitment. Jesus gave us that example on the cross. Commitment helps a woman feel secure.

Ladies, do you realize that if we show respect and honor to our husbands it's much easier for them to love and cherish us? When your man doesn't show you he cares about you as a person or if you have no voice with him, or he makes you feel like your ideas, desires, happiness or dreams don't matter, it is difficult to show respect, but it is the right thing to do—even when your husband acts selfishly. Colossians 3:18 says, *Wives, submit to your own husbands, as is fitting in the Lord.*

Gentlemen, when your woman is acting like other things are more important than you, uncaring, when she is belligerent, negative or sarcastic, it's difficult to reach out lovingly, but it's the right thing to do—even when she is acting defensively. 1 Peter 3:7 cautions, *Husbands, likewise, dwell with* them *with understanding, giving honor to the wife, as to the weaker vessel, and as* being *heirs together of the grace of life, that your prayers may not be hindered.* Don't let anything keep your prayers from being heard.

Following God's instructions forms a continuous circle. If that circle of love isn't working in your home, somebody has to mend it. So men, either you're going to need to start loving your wife so she can respect you, or ladies you're going to have to start respecting your husband so he can love you more. Somebody's got to break the cycle and mend the circle of love.

Pleasant words are like a honeycomb, sweetness to the soul and health to the body. (Proverbs 16:24 RSV.) Consider the impact of your words. How can you use them to build up and not destroy?

I guess the real question is: How much do we really want a happy marriage, a content and satisfying relationship? Do we want it enough to humble ourselves and make the necessary changes or would we rather wallow in our pride and misery? We may need to extend mercy to each other as well as forgiveness.

The Bible tells us that we can approach God at the throne of grace with boldness in Hebrews 4:16, *Let us therefore come boldly to the throne of grace, that we may obtain mercy and find grace to help in time of need.* His arms are open to us. He wants us to turn to Him for help. He wants to help us! No matter what wrong we have done, He extends mercy and grace to us because His love is inexhaustible. If we are to become more like Jesus and do things His way, we need to follow His example—show each other mercy and grace.

What does "mercy" mean? I looked it up in a dictionary. There were many definitions: compassion, pity, love, forgiveness, kindness, sympathy, tolerance, generosity, tenderheartedness. There is much God is willing to pour out on us—or open to us—however you want to look at it, if we are willing to come to Him. How would it be in our relationships if we saturated our partner with all the components of mercy?

These scriptures reminded me of how important marriage is to the Lord. He gives us the formula for a happy marriage, if we are just willing to heed His instructions. It isn't that difficult if we let God work through us and enable us to do our part in strengthening and healing our relationships. We can adhere without reservation and reap immeasurable rewards. In fact, the closer we grow to God, the closer we grow to each other—like a triangle with God at the top point. We grow more like Him and it closes the gap between us, filling both with a light and joyful heart. All we have to do is put on Jesus—in other words—let Jesus live through you!!!

If you know Jesus, your circumstances will not destroy you—break your heart, confuse you, or tempt you; but they will demand a supernatural strength from you. Even though you may be battered and broken, Jesus will care for your wounds and make a way for your restoration and healing. Your spouse may not desire you, but our Lord does. He loves you with an everlasting love, an unconditional love, a love that longs for a deep relationship with Him.

but they who wait for the LORD shall renew their strength, they shall mount up with wings like eagles, they shall run and not be weary, they shall walk and not faint.—Isaiah 40:31 RSV.

Love Overflowed:

Jesus came to my rescue. He has helped me through difficult times and He will do the same for you. Love Jesus and let Him love you. When we are alone and desperate, He is our only hope. Actually, Jesus is our only hope—anytime! God's love is always there. Extend mercy and grace in your relationships and watch what God will do for you. You have a choice as to how you will respond. He honored my willingness and now I am blessed with a wonderful marriage and a man that loves and cherishes me too!

If you are alone, you might think you need to replace Jesus for human love, but if you will give Him a chance, you will find He is enough—more than enough! He will surprise you with His care if you learn to lean on Him.

When we are younger and we feel as though life is yet ahead of us, we have dreams of getting married—of marital bliss, of meeting at the altar dressed in our best on our special day with all our friends and family present to celebrate with us.

With Love Overflowing

But weddings aren't marriages. Marriage—successful marriage—takes dedication and work. It isn't uncommon to have to "fight" for your marriage—to determine that you're going to stick it out and make it work, to keep loving no matter what.

Remember, *the devil comes to steal, kill and destroy.* If he can break up your marriage and destroy you, he conquers. Don't let him win.

For we have not a high priest who is unable to sympathize with our weaknesses, but one who in every respect has been tempted as we are, yet without sin.—Hebrews 4:15 RSV.

No matter what issues you are struggling with—if it's rejection issues from being pushed aside, mistreated, overlooked or ignored, you need to deal with them. The best way to deal with them is to understand how important you are to God and how much He loves you. Once you understand that, ask God to release you from the stronghold of rejection and replace it with the total acceptance that Christ alone offers. Please read the following story, "When Grace Abounds" for scriptural support of this and to learn who you are in Christ and how much He loves you.

Hold onto the following Bible promise from Isaiah 54:4-6, *"Do not fear, for you will not be ashamed; Neither be disgraced, for you will not be put to shame; For you will forget the shame of your youth, And will not remember the reproach of your widowhood anymore. For your Maker is your husband, The LORD of hosts is His name; And your Redeemer is the Holy One of Israel; He is called the God of the whole earth. For the LORD has called you Like a woman forsaken and grieved in spirit, ..." Says your God.* God will see you through.

If your marriage can use an extra boost, I encourage you to consider taking a marriage education class at one of the local churches that provides such instruction, or contact me and we will assist you.

Let us then with confidence draw near to the throne of grace, that we may receive mercy and find grace to help in time of need.—Hebrews 4:16 RSV

When Grace Abounds

Many of us have had times in our lives when we struggle with our value as a person. We have let the actions and opinions of others determine our worth. We have not had the opportunity, or we haven't taken advantage of the invitation, to acquaint ourselves with God and His truth of our value. When our worth is determined by the God Who created us, the One Who created us in His image, Who called us into being with a plan and purpose designated for us alone, only then can we begin to comprehend that their must be more to what we are than the opinion of others. While others make us feel insignificant, God says we are very significant. Who shall we believe? Who can we trust?

It is important to our life here on earth and our eternal life that we understand the all-encompassing, unconditional love of God, of Jesus Christ our Savior and Redeemer, of the Holy Spirit our Counselor, Comforter and Guide. We must understand, know and believe, who we are in Christ and the authority we have as a believer.

Jesus not only left heaven and came to earth to live as we live, to show us that we can be overcomers; He sacrificed and suffered to pay for our sins. We may have consequences

201

for our sins, but *If we confess our sins, He is faithful and just to forgive us our sins and to cleanse us from all unrighteousness.* (1 John 1:9)

*This is a faithful saying and worthy of all acceptance, that Christ Jesus came into the world to save sinners, of whom I am chief. However, for this reason I obtained mercy, that in me first Jesus Christ might show all long-suffering, as a pattern to those who are going to believe on Him for ever-lasting life. Now to the **King** eternal, immortal, invisible, to **God** who alone is wise, be honor and glory forever and ever. Amen.*
—1 Timothy 1:15-17.

Do you see in the scripture above that God is the **King**? Now look at the following scripture: 1 John 3:1, *Behold what manner of love the Father has bestowed on us, that **we should be called children of God!** ...*

He is the **King**! And the **King** calls us **His children**. The son of a **King** is a **Prince**. The daughter is a **Princess**. We are **royalty**! His **special treasure**!!! Scripture says, *For you are a holy people to the* LORD *your God: the* LORD *your **God has chosen you to be a people for Himself, a special treasure** above all the peoples on the face of the earth.* (Deuteronomy 7:6.)

*But you are a **chosen** generation, a **royal** priesthood, a **holy** nation. His **own special** people; that you may proclaim the praises of Him who called you out of darkness into His marvelous light.*—1 Peter 2:9.

Jesus is relational. Learn to love and trust Him. No matter how old you are He promises in Isaiah 46:4, *Even to your old age, I am He, And even to gray hairs I will carry you! I have made, and I will bear; Even I will carry, and will deliver you.*

Love Overflowed:

When we become cognizant of how His grace abounds and our awareness of His abundant love increases, we move from despair to hope.

He is God. He is King. He calls us His children. We are royalty because our Dad is King. We are His treasure, holy, chosen, His own special child. Hold your head high and walk in that!!!

202

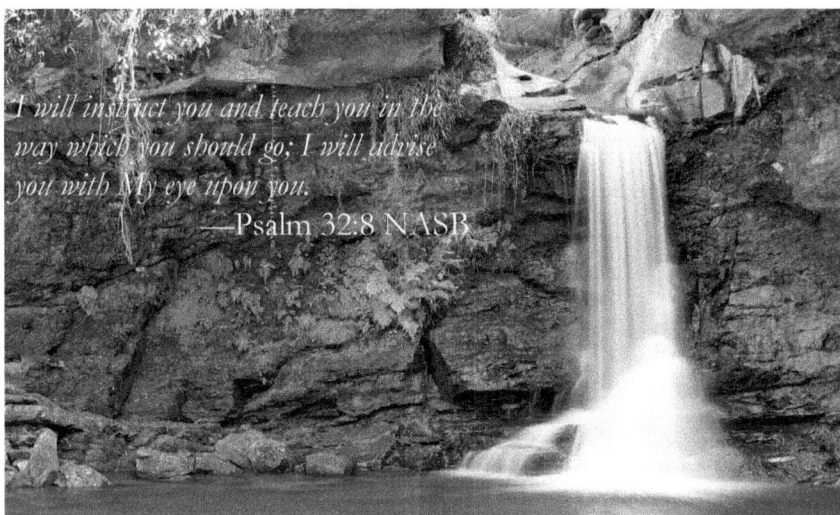

Win Me Over

God understands broken hearts. He encourages loyalty. He is pleased with surrendered obedience that trusts in His direction and plans.

I came from California to New Hampshire because God had chosen this as my new home. He gave me affirming directions through the scripture in Genesis 12:1-3, *Now the* LORD *had said to Abram* [Derry]*: "Get out of your country, From your family And from your father's house, To a land that I will show you. I will make you a great nation; I will bless you And make your name great; And you shall be a blessing. I will bless those who bless you, And I will curse him who curses you; And in you all the families of the earth shall be blessed."*

The draw to New Hampshire was the husband God had also chosen for me. He is a pastor. He, his family, and his church family came to me broken and hurting. He had lost his wife of 43 years. She had died from cancer. She was dearly loved by the church. Because of their loyalty to the "pastoral" family, it was going to be difficult for them to open their arms and hearts to me.

With Love Overflowing

My heart felt sensitive to their feelings, but I was also cautious and protective of my own heart, wondering how I was going to do living within a group of people who were resistant to my arrival.

God knew their hearts and needs and He knew my heart and needs. He understood my loneliness in a new community where I knew no one, not even my husband, well. I prayed that God would help me be compassionate to each person as I met them and would give me the right words to speak to each one.

My first introduction was to my husband's late wife Donna's sister, who was also the church secretary. She simply nodded then walked away as she stated simply, "This is going to be hard for me."

I reassured her that it was alright. Not to rush it. Take her time. I trusted the Bible promise in Deuteronomy 31:6 RSV. Its words gave me courage and hope. *Be strong and of good courage, do not fear or be in dread of them: for it is the LORD your God who goes with you; he will not fail you or forsake you.*

Then I met Julie—middle-aged and determined! Julie stood in front of me with her arms folded across her chest, feet separated and firmly planted. She looked me in the eye and stated firmly, "I am a Donna fan. If you win me over, you'll have everybody!"

I smiled and nodded, "Good to know!"

I couldn't help but smile in amusement. Julie was so cute and she actually won my heart right then.

Hmmm, things weren't going to be easy!

About a week after I met her, still anxious to become a part of the church family, God set us all up for relationship.

My husband's administrator, who was best friends with his secretary and had also been close to his wife, also seemed resistant. She looked at me with suspicion and disapproval.

We were at a Women's Ministry event and she walked up to me with a challenge, "We have a woman down in the ladies room. Maybe you better come pray for her." Her tone suggested she didn't expect any results if I did pray.

Being a chaplain and used to praying on the spot, I headed for the ladies room off the foyer. I was met by an older woman, a "Pillar of the church" guarding the door. I shared that I had been informed that a lady was down. With her arms crossed over her chest and feet planted solidly, she said, "I think we have enough people in there."

I didn't argue because just as she finished her statement, God whispered, "There's another entrance." Then He led me around and down the hall until we were at the back door to the ladies room.

I went in and found the administrator, secretary, Julie and her mother. Julie's mother was on the ground. Julie's mom was also a Donna fan—very close friends. I stepped over her body and asked Julie if I could pray. She said, "Yes." As I knelt down beside her mother, God directed me to place my hand on her forehead—something I don't usually do.

With my hand on her forehead I began to pray whatever God gave me to say. The EMTs came in as I finished my prayer and took her away to the hospital.

The next day—Sunday, Julie came up to me at church, excited. I asked about her mom. She looked at me and said, "It's amazing. When Mom came to, she asked who had prayed for her. I told her a lot of people had been praying for her. She said, 'No. Who put their hand on my forehead? When she prayed for me my death wish was gone and I was better.'

That experience opened up Julie's heart and her mother's to me, as well as many others in the church as the story began circulating. I never could have orchestrated or planned any way for people to open their hearts to me so completely, but God did it for us in just moments. I say He did it for us, because we all needed each other and still do.

Another sweet thing Jesus did was to use me to knit the church family closer together—in a fun and innovative way. I

With Love Overflowing

would meet someone, try to remember their name, and ask them someone else's name. I would often get, "I don't know" as my answer. Then God gave me a wonderful idea.

When I asked who someone was and got, "I don't know," I would then question how long they had attended the church. It was usually many years. My next query was how long the person I had originally asked about had been attending. The answer usually came back, "Oh, I think they have been attending here a long time."

Then I would assure them, "Since you don't know their name, I will find out and tell you. No one expects me to know everyone's name. You tell me who you know and I'll tell you the names of those I meet."

Pretty soon the whole church knew each other and were calling each other by name. God is so much fun!

Love Overflowed:

I love this church family with every bit of me. God has blessed us by many experiences that have "knit" us together. He even woke up the "pillar of the church" and showed her what I was going through and had her praying for me for two hours in the middle of the night.

And we know that all things work together for good to those who love God, to those who are the called according to His purpose.
—Romans 8:28.

You never have to doubt or question God. He loves us so much. God knows we all need each other and He knows how to strengthen love and appreciation among us.

Do you know that you need not fear because God can and will make a way for you? To make friends you need to prove yourself friendly. What are you doing to break down the walls? Are you reaching out to others or waiting for others to reach out to you?

206

In that day the LORD Almighty will be a glorious crown,
a beautiful wreath for the remnant of his people.
—Isaiah 28:5 NIV

Wreath—God's Crown

When I was alone, after God had directed me to purchase our home from my husband, He asked me to dedicate the house to Him. I asked Jesus what He wanted me to do. He revealed a very special plan, a beautiful ceremony. I was to invite some of my close pastor friends along with their spouses and ask each of them to bring to the ceremony whatever God put in their hearts.

I prepared a small thank-you gift for each of them, a candle with a note thanking them for sharing their light and love. I had snacks and goodies prepared for the celebration after the dedication ceremony.

The night before the anticipated date, I was leaving work to go home. I sat in my car a moment and said, "Lord, is there any thing else I need for tomorrow evening? I have to get it tonight if there is. I won't have time after work tomorrow night. I will have to hurry back home for company." I waited and listened.

I sensed God was directing me to go to Michael's, a craft shop. I asked God what we were going to get. No answer. I drove to Michael's still praying, got out of the car, grabbed a shopping cart and entered the store. I stood inside looking around. Again I prayed.

God began directing me around the store. We picked up a wreath, some ivy and small battery-operated white lights to wrap around it. I assumed it might need a ribbon and bow. What else? I turned to look around and here came a gal from the hospital. She greeted me asking what I was doing. I explained.

"What a lovely idea," she replied. "Are you putting any birds on the wreath symbolizing 'new beginnings?'"

I hadn't thought of that, but I did believe God was leading in this. I got the birds and followed further impression on my heart. I picked up a nest and some plastic eggs that looked quite real. The last things I sensed I was to get were white flowers to symbolize a pure and sanctified environment.

When I got home I spread everything out and asked God how He wanted it put together. God gave me the idea of splitting the eggs half way and placing them in the nest. It was a deep nest and held many eggs. I was to give each participant coming to the dedication a small piece of paper and ask them to write a blessing on it for our home, then fold it up and stick it in an egg.

It was a lovely service. The pastors all walked through the house consecrating it to the Lord and anointing each room. Then we joined together in the living room where God had given one of the pastors the song "Bless This House" for us to sing together. Then another pastor read scripture and prayed. Another pastor sat a chair in the middle of the room and one at a time had each of us who lived there sit in the chair and receive a prayer of blessing. Then the papers and eggs were passed out. After the blessings were written on them, they were placed in the eggs and nestled in the nest. It was a treasured time with special memories, even as I reflect on it today.

A few days later God blessed me further by giving me the text listed at the beginning of the story, Isaiah 28:5 NIV, *In that day the LORD Almighty will be a glorious crown, a beautiful wreath for the remnant of his people.* A wreath—God's crown!

The wreath has a significant meaning. Its circular shape represents eternity, because it has no beginning and no end. From a Christian perspective, it represents an unending circle of life. The Bible refers to a garland, a wreath and a crown as all similar.

Love Overflowed:

God Himself explains the meaning of this wreath in the Word of God. Thank You God for Your seal on Your people; for Your love poured out without being solicited and for Your blessings over our home with the promise that You have given us "new beginnings."

For I know the plans I have for you," declares the LORD, "plans to prosper you and not to harm you, plans to give you hope and a future.
—Jeremiah 29:11 NIV.

Every day can be a day of new beginnings. Is this your day? Have you ever considered praying through your house asking God to cleanse it from any evil; to purify and sanctify it?

Invite Him in to dwell in your home and live in your heart. If that's difficult to understand—just try it. Right now say, Jesus I choose You. Please come dwell in me. Take my life and guide me to fill Your plans. Cleanse my home from any evil and take up residency there. In Jesus' name, Amen

If this prayer was your first invitation to Jesus, it is important for you to read to the end of this book.

With Love Overflowing

Seek Ye First The Kingdom Of God
—Helen Steiner Rice[†]

Life is a mixture of sunshine and rain,
Good things and bad things, pleasure and pain,
We can't have all sunshine, but it's certainly true
There is never a cloud the sun doesn't shine through …
So always remember that whatever betide you,
The power of God is always beside you,
And if friends disappoint you and plans go astray
And nothing works out in just the right was
And you feel you have failed in achieving your goal,
And that life wrongly placed you in an unfitting role,
Take heart and "stand-tall" and think who you are,
For God is your Father and no one can bar
Or keep you from reaching your desired success,
Or withhold the joy that is yours to possess …
For with God on your side, it matters not who
Is working to keep life's good things from you,
For you need nothing more than God's guidance and love
To insure you the things that you're most worthy of …
So trust in His wisdom and follow His ways,
And be not concerned with the world's empty praise,
But seek *first His Kingdom* and you will possess
The world's greatest riches which is true happiness.

†©1967 Helen Steiner Rice Foundation Fund, LLC, a wholly owned subsidiary
of Cincinatti Museum Center

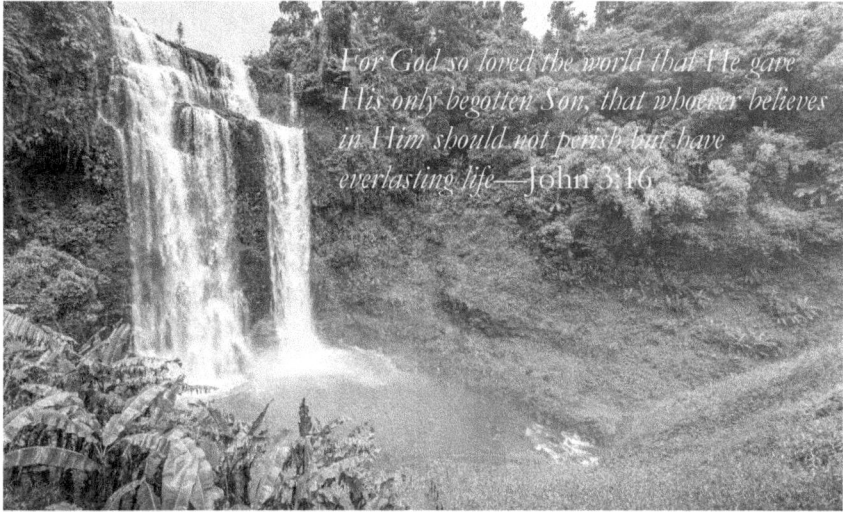

For God so loved the world that He gave His only begotten Son, that whoever believes in Him should not perish but have everlasting life—John 3:16

Your God Loves You

My stories reveal the extravagant, overflowing love of an incomprehensible and irresistible God. I want to talk more about that love and our hope.

The Bible says in John 14:6-7, *Jesus said to him, "I am the way, and the truth, and the life. No one comes to the Father except through Me. If you had known Me, you would have known My Father also; and from now on you know Him and have seen Him."* As we understand more about Jesus we will also become more acquainted with our Father in heaven. Sooo, let's talk about Jesus, because He is the way, the truth and the life! Some insights:

In John 1:5 ESV we are told, *The light shines in the darkness, and the darkness has not overcome it.* Other Bible versions say, *the darkness can never extinguish it.* What does that mean? It means several things, looking at it from different perspectives. First there is the obvious—if you are in a dark room and you put on the light—it's light. Darkness has not overcome the light. Now look at this verse from a more spiritual viewpoint. It means that when we have the light of God in us and we are among others that have not yet experienced Him, our lives will shine out as different and will expose the "dark side," the evil

211

around us. Now one step farther—Jesus is that light! The Bible tells us in John 8:12 *Then Jesus spoke to them again, saying, "I am the light of the world. He who follows Me shall not walk in darkness, but have the light of life."* He is the "light of the world." So as Jesus shows up in any given situation, He casts His brilliance, His light, in the midst of the darkness or evil around Him and if we follow Him, we will have that light of life as well!

We are promised to be overcomers! There is hope for our future right now! We are taught in Hebrews 4:14-15 NRSV, *Since, then, we have a great high priest who has passed through the heavens, Jesus, the Son of God, let us hold fast to our confession. For we do not have a high priest who is unable to sympathize with our weaknesses, but we have one who in every respect has been tested as we are, yet without sin.* Wow!!! Do you understand what this is saying? Jesus, the Son of God understands what we are going through because He endured it when He was here on earth. He was tested and passed! He did not sin. He did not give in to the temptation to be less than loving and accepting. He experienced and dealt in love and patience with the broken, sinful people around Him that were trying to destroy, demean, discredit and kill Him.

But it gets better! The Bible tells us that we can approach God at the throne of grace with boldness in Hebrews 4:16, *Let us therefore approach the throne of grace with boldness, so that we may receive mercy and find grace to help in time of need.* His arms are open to us. He wants us to turn to Him for help. He wants to help us! No matter what wrong we have done He extends mercy and grace to us.

What does "mercy" mean? I looked it up in the dictionary. There were many definitions: compassion, pity, love, forgiveness, kindness, sympathy, tolerance, generosity, tenderheartedness. There is a lot God is willing to pour out on us— or open to us—however you want to look at it, if we are willing to come to Him.

Here is what the dictionary says about grace: In western Christian theology, grace is the love and mercy given to us by

God because God desires us to have it, not because of anything we have done to earn it. It is not a created substance of any kind. It is an attribute of God that is most manifest in the salvation of sinners.

God extending mercy and grace to us opens the way for the past to be put behind and new opportunities for our present and future. We have a God Who loves us, has overcome the wickedness of the world on our behalf, wants to be in relationship with us and help us be victorious, too.

In Matthew 6:8 NRSV, ... *your Father knows what you need before you ask him.* And in Matthew 6:33, *But seek first the kingdom of God and his righteousness, and all these things shall be added to you.* Jesus—God the Father—Holy Spirit—have their eyes on you! They know what you need before you ask. God is just waiting for you to ask. And when we seek the Kingdom of God and His righteousness (right doing in our life), He is going to take care of everything we need. When our hearts turn to Him, even before we call, the Father has already begun putting into motion whatever is needed to provide for us and bless us.

We can only know how intimately God loves us and knows each of us when we pray. When we come and pour out our heart needs to Him specifically and then experience His answers to our cries. God wants us to come to Him with our needs, Matthew 7:7: *Ask, and it will be given to you; seek, and you will find; knock, and it will be opened to you.*

Our heavenly Father knows exactly what we need and what is best for us. He wants to show us that when we are weak, He is strong. Philippians 4:13: *I can do all things through Christ who strengthens me.* When we are discouraged He is our hope. When we have needs, He wants to bless us. When we feel unloved, He will show us how much He loves us.

Speaking of how much he loves us, it is hard to take it in. It is especially hard for us to accept if we have had unhealthy relationships with our parents or betrayal and rejection from our companions. But God is different. His love is never failing and He always wants what is best for us. Because we are His, He loves us, even with our imperfections and brokenness.

Jesus is calling today. He wants to call us from darkness to marvelous light. He wants us to know that His love never stops—it is overflowing. If you will open your heart today, if you will invite Him in, if you will pray—talk to Him— experience Him, you will find that This Jesus, This God, is truly irresistible!!! Don't wait. Do it now. Give God a chance.

©2021 Danny Hahlbohm, www.inspiredart.store

Now acquaint yourself with Him, and be at peace; Thereby good will come to you. Receive, please, instruction from His mouth, And lay up His words in your heart. If you return to the Almighty, you will be built up; You will remove iniquity far from your tents. … You will make your prayer to Him, He will hear you, …—Job 22:21-23, 27.

Epilogue

Now you know more about me than I know about you! I hope you will go to the end of this book, follow the information and share about yourself and how this book has spoken to you.

Sharing these stories of God's grace and love has been written not only to bring you hope and increase your understanding of Who God is but also to glorify God, give honor to Jesus, and express appreciation to the Holy Spirit. With David in Psalm 40:9-10, I declare, *I have proclaimed the good news of righteousness In the great assembly; Indeed, I do not restrain my lips, O* LORD, *You Yourself know. I have not hidden Your righteousness within my heart; I have declared Your faithfulness and Your salvation; I have not concealed Your lovingkindness and Your truth From the great assembly.*

I believe strongly in accountability partnerships. When you have trusting relationships, it is easier to share truthfully, from the heart, without reservation. We learn from each other and sharing gives us an awareness of how we really feel or how we are actually responding to situations in life. If the mistakes I have made in my life will prevent you from having to go through similar consequences, it will have been worth my sharing with transparency.

If any story I recorded here will heighten your awareness of a loving God Who will walk by your side through any circumstance of your life or has encouraged you to accept Him as the Lord of your life, then that is reward enough for my time spent. I hope you will share any life changes you have incurred with me.

If you are interested in more of my inspirational stories, you will enjoy the companions to this book, *With Gladness Every Day* and *With Kisses From Heaven.*

Maybe you haven't met Jesus yet and would like the assurance that He also knows **your** name. To develop that personal relationship and learn how to pray effectively, I encourage you to look into my books *Praying in the "Yes" of God* and *Growing in the "Yes" of God.*

If you are convinced you would like to have things different in your life, coming in the next few pages is a sinner's prayer and Prayer of Commitment. I invite you to read "Meaning Of Commitment To God" and take this opportunity to secure your new or renewed commitment to God by reading through the prayers, prayerfully initialing each paragraph you agree with and then signing at the end.

God will keep His word. May He bless you on your continued spiritual journey.

Looking forward to meeting in heaven,

Derry

… For from the overflow of the heart the mouth speaks.
—Matthew 12:34 TLV.

You have kept your promise to your servant David, my father. You made that promise with your own mouth, and with your own hands you have fulfilled it today.—1 Kings 8:24 NLT.

Meaning Of Commitment To God

This **Sinner's Prayer**, when prayed in faith, is met with the love and grace of God Who gives the free gift of eternal life to the one who prays. Eternal life is a life with God that begins right here on earth and continues with God in heaven for eternity. The moment you pray you will be born again by the Holy Spirit (John 3:1-21). You will be a new person with a new identity. This may sound too good to be true but I assure you, if anything, I am understating the life and adventures that you can look forward to as you begin your journey with the Lord Jesus Christ and your fellow Christ followers.

Before you pray let's look at what the Bible has to say. For those who have read my book and are not familiar with the Bible, you should know the Bible is also referred to as the Holy Scriptures and the Word of God. It is a record of the relationship of God with mankind. The Bible is not like any other book ever written in the history of mankind, for it reveals the love of the one true God, the Creator of the heavens and the earth and seas and all that is in them, for the world and His desire to have a special people who will know Him and love Him.

The problem is sin. What is sin? The New Testament word for *sin* originates from a Greek term used in archery meaning to "miss the mark," the bullseye. If we are honest we all miss doing what we know is right at times. After all, we are only human and we do the best we can. Unfortunately the best we can doesn't meet the standard of a holy and righteous God.

There is a way that seems *right to a man, But its end* is *the way of death.*—Proverbs 14:12.

Therefore you shall be perfect, just as your Father in heaven is perfect.
—Matthew 5:48.

For the wages of sin is death, but the gift of God is eternal life in Christ Jesus our Lord.—Romans 6:23.

for all have sinned and fall short of the glory of God,—Romans 3:23.

God's standard is perfection, Matthew 5:48: *Therefore you shall be perfect, just as your Father in heaven is perfect.* and it is not possible for anyone to obtain perfection apart from Christ. The only perfect person is Jesus Christ the Son of God. He imparts His robe of righteousness to cover our sins.

For God so loved the world that He gave His only begotten Son, that whoever believes in Him shall not perish but have everlasting life.
—John 3:16.

Jesus said to him, "I am the way, the truth, and the life. No one comes to the Father except through Me.—John 14:6.

Jesus took the punishment for our sins when He suffered and died on the cross. There is no other Lord or Savior.

But what does it say? "The word is near you, in your mouth and in your heart" (that is, the word of faith which we preach): that if you confess with your mouth the Lord Jesus and believe in your heart that God has raised Him from the dead, you will be saved. For with the heart one believes unto righteousness, and with the mouth confession is made unto salvation.—Romans 10:8-10.

Accepting Jesus does not mean things in your life will be without trial or tribulation; but when you face them, you will have the assurance God is by your side and will see you through.

Do you believe Jesus is the Son of God Who died for your sins? Do you believe God raised Him from the dead? If you do, pray this simple prayer:

A Sinner's Prayer

Father God, I believe that Jesus Christ is Lord and Savior. I believe you sent your Son Jesus Who died for my sins. I believe that He was raised from the dead.

Father God, I ask you to forgive my sins. Lord Jesus I ask you to come into my heart and be my Lord and Savior. I thank you for hearing my prayer and for saving me and giving me eternal life.

Father God, I ask you to fill me with the Holy Spirit and empower me to live the life you have called me to.

In Jesus' Name, Amen.

Now that you have placed your trust in Jesus Christ, let me encourage you to read the Bible and let God work His Word into your heart. Remember you are not the same person you once were. Until now the world and circumstances have defined you. But now you have been born again; you are a new creation handcrafted by God. I encourage you to let God lead you to a Bible-based church that will teach you Truth from the Word of God and prepare you to be baptized as one of God's followers (disciples).

Therefore, if anyone is in Christ, he is a new creation; old things have passed away; behold, all things have become new.—2 Corinthians 5:17.

Christians are meant to have the same vocation as their King, that of cross-bearers. It is this conscience of a high calling and of partnership with Jesus which brings gladness in tribulations.

—Richard Wurmbrand

While faith makes all things possible, it is love that makes all things easy.

— Evan H. Hopkins

Prayer Of Commitment

Father God, Lord Jesus, Blessed Holy Spirit;

Thank You for Your unconditional and sacrificial love for me. I desire to live out Your divine plan intended specifically for me.

Thank You that Jesus died that I may live. I choose this day to ask for forgiveness of my sins and accept Jesus' sacrifice on the cross for me.

I want You as Lord of my life and to live a life of answered prayer, walking in Your will, empowered by Your Holy Spirit. I will serve You gladly with wholehearted appreciation for all You have given, all You have done, and all that You offer.

I commit to live my life to honor You, my Lord. By Your grace, I will follow Your example. Help me become familiar with scripture, presenting the promises for fulfillment as I work in partnership with You. With joy I will share with others what God does for me, with me, and in me. Use me to love and influence souls for the glory of the Kingdom.

On this, the _____ day of _____, 20___, I choose to surrender my life to You; to offer my heart for Your dwelling place, and to follow wherever You lead me.

Signature: _____

Only Two Religions

While presenting the Gospel on the street of a California city, we were often interrupted about as follows: "Look here, sir! There are hundreds of religions in this country, and the followers of each sect think theirs the only right one. How can poor plain men like us find out what really is the truth?"

We generally replied something like this: "Hundreds of religions, you say? That's strange; I've heard of only two."

"Oh, but you surely know there are more than that?"

"Not at all, sir. I find, I admit, many shades of difference in the opinions of those comprising the two great schools; but after all there are but two. The one covers all who expect salvation by doing; the other, all who have been saved by something done. So you see the whole question is very simple. Can you save yourself, or must you be saved by another? If you can be your own savior, you do not need my message. If you cannot, you may well listen to it."

—H.A. Ironside,
Gospel Herald

... choose for yourselves this day whom you will serve, ...
—Joshua 24:15.

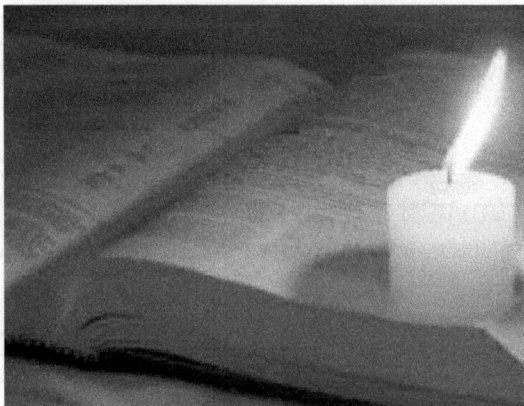

Titles by Dr. Derry James-Tannariello

For gift or bulk orders of these, or any of Derry's books, please visit our website:

FreedomInSurrender.net

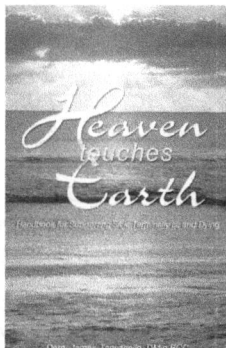

Heaven Touches Earth—Handbook for Supporting Sick, Terminally Ill and Dying *was written to provide you with the skills and tools necessary to bring solace and comfort to the sick and suffering at home, in the hospital or hospice ministry.*

This concise "how-to handbook" is also a succinct resource of clear insight into hospital practices and protocols useful in training volunteers, parish visitors, pastors and chaplains and a helpful refresher guide for those who have studied hospital ministry.

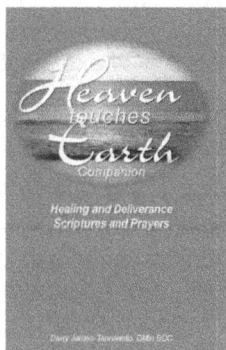

Heaven Touches Earth Companion—Healing and Deliverance Scriptures and Prayers *is a take-along resource containing only the* Healing and Deliverance Scriptures and Prayers *chapter of the* Heaven Touches Earth *book. It is designed for those ministering in a supportive role (63 pages).*

Also available in eBook format at Amazon.com, or at

FreedomInSurrender.net

Living Volumes One and Two:

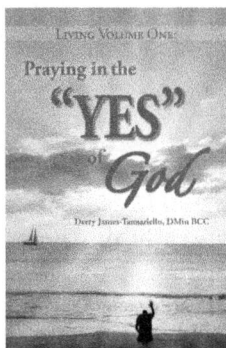

Praying in the "YES" of God

God knows your name! *Do you believe that? Do you believe there even is a God?*

Do you believe Jesus Christ knows who you are and is interested in your life? Do you believe He is Who He says He is, and can do what He says He can do?

When you pray, does it sometimes feel like your prayers are hitting the ceiling, or are falling on deaf ears? Are you angry with God because your prayers seem not to be answered? Have you given up asking God for things for yourself because you don't want to be disappointed again; or you're afraid if God is silent you will begin to question His existence, and then you'll have nothing to put your hope and trust in?

Praying in the "YES" of God *will help you find those answers and give you the tools to face the unknown with the peace and confidence that God loves you! Learn how to live with triumphant faith, peace of mind, and enthusiastic testimony.*

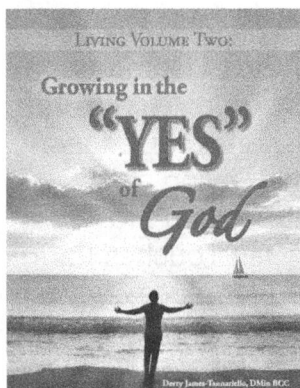

Growing in the "YES" of God

God Has a Plan for Your Life! *Do you wonder why it seems some people have answers to their prayers and unexplainable miracles in their life—and you don't? Is there really any such thing as security and joy? What does love mean? What if you could find the answers to these questions and more? You can.*

This in-depth Bible Study on principles of a more effective prayer life, further growth in Jesus and living out His character and plans for your life victoriously and blessed will reassure you of God's love. It is best understood and most effective if preceded by Living Volume One: Praying in the "YES" of God.

Also available in eBook format at Amazon.com, or at

FreedomInSurrender.net

Three companion books:

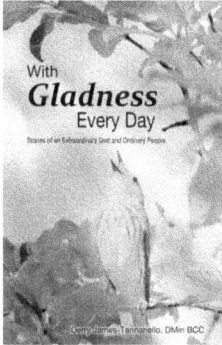

With Gladness Every Day

Become confident in your walk with God and increase your trust and hope in Him. The stories in this book are answers to prayers and lessons from life experiences dependent on God's grace and mercy.

In this time of uncertainty and turmoil in our nation, are you mindful of the magnificence of God's love and the countless ways He expresses it to you each day? If not, it's time to reconnect to God's presence and awaken your senses to His unconditional, all encompassing love for **you**.

Be inspired by these stories, and let them arouse in you a desire to become acquainted with this King of kings, or renew your desire to commit all to Him and sing His praises!!!

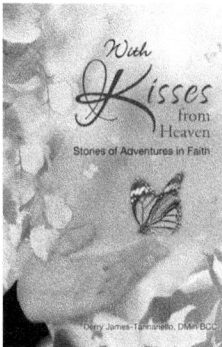

With Kisses From Heaven

Even in times of uncertainty, love produces a heart of gratitude. With a thankful and adoring heart we notice the small as well as the larger things done for us—out of love and devotion to us.

God is continually doing and giving for us; for our best interest, for our delight, for our care and pleasure—to offer encouragement, protection and provision, or make life easier.

But always, always, it is to let us know He is there, right by our side, attentive and aware of everything that concerns us, pouring out love in unexpected ways. I call these surprises "Kisses from Heaven."

I pray that by sharing some of my experiences of God's intervention and lessons learned that punctuate particular Scriptures, you will become more aware of how attentive God is to you. May your heart burst with appreciation and may your love for Him increase. May your faith grow and keep you steadfast when the trials of life attempt to overwhelm you.

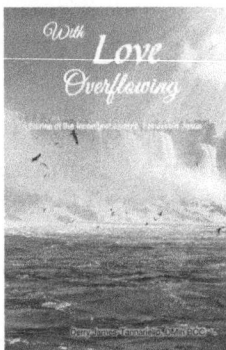

With Love Overflowing

God's abiding love is ever present. He offers a place of peace, hope for the future and freedom from fear. Every day is a new day of life and opportunities; challenges and joys. In this world of insecurity, we are looking for dependable security and unconditional love. The nature of life is such that conflict—inner and outer—is inevitable. Can we find peace, security and love amidst conflict? The answer is Yes! We can find it all in the overflowing love of God in Christ Jesus.

I pray these stories will open your eyes to the many ways God has proven Himself present in your life and confirm there is hope in Jesus during life's turmoil and storms. Our God of love is a personal, caring God Who loves extravagantly with overwhelming, incomprehensible love. He pours out His love on us and will use us to let others experience His love through us. He is there for you, even in silence. When you become aware of that, He will become irresistible to you too and you will desire to be more like Him.

Also available in eBook format at Amazon.com, or at

FreedomInSurrender.net

Upcoming Title:

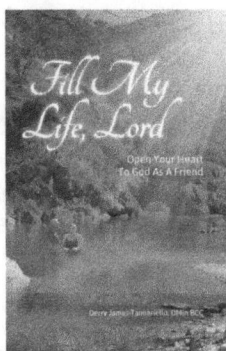

Fill My Life, Lord

What **fills** your mind, your heart, your home and your life depends upon what you allow to **fill** your hands.

The stories in the Bible are not just stories to inspire and encourage you, but stories to build your relationship with God and change your life. What He has done in the past He will do for you in the present.

If you don't have a personal relationship with God, I invite you to **fill** your hands with this book and open your mind and heart to this study. The Lord is waiting and willing to **fill** your life and prove He knows you and hears you. When you take one step towards the Savior, He runs the rest of the way to meet you. May your life be transformed.

DID THIS BOOK BLESS YOU?

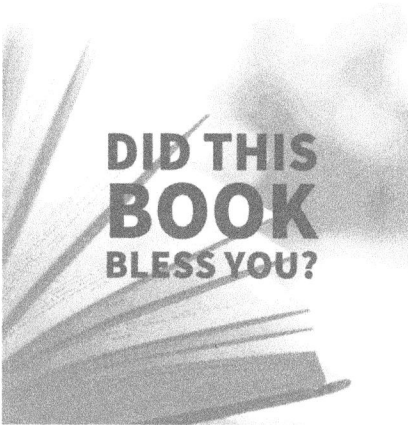

Why Not Bless Others!!!

FreedomInSurrrender.net

√ Mention this book on your social media platforms.

√ Are you a blogger? Consider writing a book review on your blog. Post it to your blog and other retail book outlets.

√ Know someone else who would be blessed by this book? Pick up a copy for a friend or coworker

√ Recommend this book to your church library or small group study.

√ Share this message on Facebook. "I was blessed by **With Love Overflowing** by Derry James-Tannariello and Freedom In Surrender Ministries."

Scan this QR code for
FreedomInSurrender.net

* 9 781735 420806 *